THE COMPLETE GIRLS' GUIDE TO PUBERTY

Understanding Your Evolving Body, Mind, and Feelings During Growth | Girls Puberty Book Aged 8-12

ELISABETH M. CAMPBELL

ISBN : 9798878889742

CONTENTS

Introduction   5

Welcome to Your Journey   5

How This Guide Can Help You   6

Chapter 1. Discovering Puberty   9

1.1 The Puberty Journey: An Overview   10

1.2 Your Personal Puberty Timeline   12

1.3 Embracing Individual Differences   16

Chapter 2. Physical Changes and Health   21

2.1 Understanding Your Body's Transformation   21

2.2 The Basics of the Female Reproductive System   23

2.3 The Stages of Breast Development   26

2.4 Dealing with New Body Hair and Skincare Tips   31

2.5 Growth Spurts: Changes in Height and Weight   35

2.6 Personal Hygiene: Caring for Your Changing Body   39

Chapter 3. Menstruation and You   43

3.1 Demystifying Menstruation   43

3.2 Preparing for Your First Period   45

3.3 Navigating Period Challenges   51

3.4 Questions and Answers About Periods   53

Chapter 4. Emotional Evolution   57

4.1 Understanding Mood Swings   57

4.2 Handling Stress and Anxiety   60

4.3 Building a Positive Body Image   65

4.4 Nurturing Healthy Friendships   68

4.5 The Impact of Social Media on Emotions   72

Chapter 5. Social Dynamics and Relationships   **75**

5.1 Family Dynamics During Puberty   75

5.2 Friendships: Old and New   78

5.3 Dealing with Bullying and Peer Pressure   81

5.4 Understanding Crushes and Romantic Feelings   85

5.5 Balancing Online and In-Person Relationships   90

Chapter 6. Cultivating Healthy Habits   **95**

6.1 The Role of Nutrition and Exercise   96

6.2 The Importance of Sleep   99

6.3 Establishing Healthy Daily Routines   102

Chapter 7. Communication and Support   **107**

7.1 How to Talk to Parents and Guardians   107

7.2 Seeking Support from Teachers and Counselors   111

7.3 Finding the Courage to Ask for Help   115

Chapter 8. Navigating Misinformation   **121**

8.1 Addressing Common Myths   121

8.2 Sorting Fact from Fiction   124

Chapter 9. Further Resources and Guidance   **127**

9.1 Recommended Reading and Websites   127

9.2 Accessing Support Networks and Helplines   129

Chapter 10. Conclusion   **133**

10.1 Embracing Your Unique Journey   133

10.2 Looking Forward with Confidence   134

Disclaimer   **137**

INTRODUCTION

☆ WELCOME TO YOUR JOURNEY

Embarking on the journey of puberty is similar to setting foot on a trail that leads to a breathtaking vista. It's a path packed with new sceneries, unexpected twists and turns, and even a few uphill battles, but the view at the end is worth every step. It's the journey towards becoming your grown-up self, and it's nothing short of magical! Just like every exciting journey, puberty brings with it changes and transformations. It's like you're a caterpillar getting ready to become a butterfly. These changes will happen to your body, your mind, and your emotions. They're all part of growing up and becoming stronger, wiser, and more mature. One of the first noticeable transformations happens to your body. It's like you've been given a key to a secret garden, and as you step in, you'll notice that things are starting to grow. You'll see changes in your height and weight. You may start to develop breasts, and eventually, you'll experience your first period. It's a sign that your body is preparing itself for the amazing capability of one day possibly becoming a mother. But it's not just the physical changes you'll notice. Your emotions will embark on their journey too. It's a bit like riding a roller coaster, where some days you might feel on top of the world, and other days it feels like you're on a speedy downhill ride. But that's normal! Your emotions are simply learning to adapt to all the changes happening inside you. And lastly, your mind will also go through a transformation. It will grow, stretch, and expand like never before. You might find that you're thinking about things in a different way or that some things that used to be important to you aren't anymore. You might start to see the world in new colors, with more complex shades and tones.

So, as you set off on this journey, remember:

☆ It's a journey that everyone goes on, so you're not alone.

☆ Every person's journey is unique, and there's no right or wrong way to experience it.

☆ It's okay to have questions or feel confused sometimes. You're learning and growing, and that's something to be proud of.

☆ This journey of transformation is a hallmark of your strength and resilience. And it's a journey that will transform you into the wonderful grown-up you're destined to be.

You're beginning an amazing adventure, and we're here to walk through it with you, every step of the way.

☆ HOW THIS GUIDE CAN HELP YOU

As you grow up, you'll experience all sorts of changes. Your body will change, your thoughts and feelings will evolve, and even your relationships with others might shift. It can be a thrilling and confusing time, and that's perfectly okay! You're not alone in this journey. To make this transition a little less puzzling, you have this guide in your hands. Imagine you're setting out on a new adventure across the wilderness. For that, you'll need a backpack full of essentials, right? This book is just like that backpack for your journey through puberty. It's packed full of invaluable resources that will help you navigate through this new, exciting phase of your life. It's like having a personal guidebook to assist you in understanding and coping with the changes you'll undergo.

This book provides you with reliable information. It's like having a trustworthy friend who knows all about the world of growing up and is ready to share their wisdom with you. All the information in this guide has been carefully researched and checked, so you can trust that what you're reading is true and accurate. This book covers a selection of topics that will help you understand the different aspects of puberty. It talks about physical changes, like growing taller, developing curves, and your first period. It also dives into emotional changes, such as mood swings and new feelings. Additionally, it explains the shifts you might notice in your social life, from friendships to first crushes. This guide offers more than just information. It provides a space for you to explore your feelings and thoughts about puberty. You might find that it sparks questions you hadn't thought of before or encourages you to think about your experiences in a different light. It's very much like having a conversation with a wise and understanding friend.

Chapter 1
DISCOVERING PUBERTY

☆ 1.1 THE PUBERTY JOURNEY: AN OVERVIEW

Take a moment to imagine yourself on an exciting journey, full of new discoveries and changes. In many ways, that's what puberty is - an adventure of growth that every girl experiences as she transforms from a child into a young woman. When we talk about puberty, we're referring to a phase in your life that's marked by a series of physical, emotional, and psychological changes. These changes are like a beautiful metamorphosis, turning caterpillars into butterflies, preparing you to become the fantastic, capable adult woman you will be one day!

Let's start with physical changes. You will see your body blossoming in different ways. You might notice your breasts beginning to develop, which is usually the first sign of puberty, and it's completely normal if one grows faster than the other in the beginning. You'll also start to grow pubic hair and, later, underarm hair. Another significant change is the start of your menstrual cycle, known as your period, which we'll delve into further in later chapters. Alongside these physical changes, you may also notice some shifts in how you feel and think. This is the emotional and psychological part of the journey. Emotionally, you might feel like you're on a roller coaster ride, with your moods swinging high and low. One moment, you could be giggling with your friends, and the next, you might feel upset or irritable. It's all part and parcel of the changes in your hormone levels. Psychologically, you'll also start to see the world in a different light. You might start to feel more self-conscious about your appearance and how others perceive you. You might also start developing crushes, which is an entirely normal part of growing up. To help visualize these changes, let's imagine them as different stages in a butterfly's transformation:

★ The Caterpillar Phase: This is before puberty starts. You're a child, enjoying your games, and don't yet notice the changes that are about to come.

★ The Cocoon Stage: This is when puberty begins. Just like a caterpillar wrapping itself in a silky cocoon, your body starts to change, and you'll see and feel a difference in your physical and emotional self.

★ The Transformation: This is the height of puberty, when your body undergoes significant changes, like your first period and changes in your shape and height.

★ The Emergence: The final stage is when you have fully grown into a young woman. Puberty has ended, but your journey of self-discovery continues.

Remember, every girl's journey through puberty is unique. Some might start their journey earlier, some later; for some it's a sprint, for others, a marathon. But regardless of when it starts or how long it takes, it's your special transformation, your personal voyage of discovery. And like every journey, it's not always smooth. There might be bumps and twists along the way, but always remember, it's a beautiful process that leads to a fantastic destination - the amazing woman you'll become!

Journal Exercise:

I. Draw a roadmap of your puberty journey so far, detailing every change that has happened in your body or mind that you've noticed. Don't forget to note down the changes you might be looking forward to, or worried about.

2. Write down five questions you have about your puberty journey after reading this chapter.

3. Write a letter to yourself two years in the future. Discuss your hopes, fears, and anticipations about going through

puberty. Discuss any misconceptions that you had before reading this chapter that are now cleared, and how this knowledge could help your future self.

4. Reflect on how you feel about the changes that puberty brings. Do these feelings change after learning more about what's happening in your body?

5. List three people you trust who you can talk to about your feelings regarding puberty. Explain why you chose them.

☆ 1.2 YOUR PERSONAL PUBERTY TIMELINE

As you grow and change, your body embarks on an amazing journey known as puberty. This journey is like a personal timeline that all girls go through, and it can be split into several stages. But, before we dive into these stages, let's first be clear - there's no rush! Each and every one of us grows at our own unique pace. What might be happening to your friend right now may happen to you later, and that is perfectly okay. Remember, your body knows what it's doing and will follow its own schedule. Let's take a closer look at the different stages most girls undergo during puberty:

1. The first sign: This stage usually begins around 8-13 years old. You might notice your breasts starting to bud, which means they're just beginning to develop. Another change could be the growth of pubic hair. You might also observe that you're growing taller or that your hips are starting to widen.

2. Developing further: This stage typically kicks in when you're between 9-15 years old. You continue to get taller, your breasts keep on developing, and your pubic hair grows thicker. You might also start to see hair under your arms.

3. The arrival of menstruation: Usually around 10-16 years old, you'll experience your first period. Don't worry if it's irregular at first - it's normal! Your body is still figuring things out.

4. Almost there: Between the ages of 12-19, your growth in height will slow down, and you'll reach your adult height. Your breasts and pubic hair will also reach their adult appearance.

5. The finishing touches: This is the final stage of puberty, which usually happens between the ages of 14-20. Your body shape will continue to become more adult-like, and

you'll notice that your menstrual cycle has become more predictable.

What's important to remember here is that these stages are just guidelines. You might skip some of these stages, or they might happen in a different order. Or you might find yourself in more than one stage at once! Puberty is a mix-and-match kind of experience, and everyone's timeline is unique. Your timeline will be different from your best friend's, your sister's, or that girl's in your class. And that's perfectly normal! In the end, it's not about keeping up with anyone else. It's about understanding and accepting the changes as they come, knowing that they're all part of your personal journey to becoming the amazing adult you're meant to be. So, embrace your personal puberty timeline — it's yours and yours alone, and there's no need to compare it with anyone else's.

Imagine you're set for a grand adventure, a journey to an unexplored land. There's excitement, yes, but also a bit of uncertainty. This is what your journey through puberty is like. It's your personal adventure, unique to you, and it won't be exactly the same as anyone else's. Let's say you're Ava, who just turned nine. You're playing with your friends when you notice your chest is a bit tender. It's the first sign that you're starting your personal puberty timeline. For Ava, it was her chest. She noticed small, tender lumps under her nipples, which were the beginnings of her breast buds. As the weeks went by, she noticed they were getting a bit bigger. It was a little uncomfortable at first, but she got used to it. If you experience something similar, remember, it's just your body signaling that it's ready to take the next step in your adventure of growing up. Let's move to another part of Ava's adventure. A few months later, Ava noticed her hair getting oilier, and she started having to wash it more often. And then, one day, she found a couple of pimples on her face. It was confusing, a little scary, but it's all part of the journey. She learned that it was because her skin was producing more oil due to hormones. So, she started washing her face twice a day with a mild soap and drinking plenty of water to keep her skin clear. Ava's mother explained to her that these changes didn't mean she would get her period right away. Puberty is a gradual process, and everyone's timeline is different. Ava's friend Mia, for example, didn't start developing breasts until she was almost 11, but she started growing underarm hair around the same time Ava did. When Ava turned 11, she started noticing a white or yellowish discharge in her underwear. It was strange and a bit scary, but Ava's mom explained to her that it was a normal part of puberty, a sign that her first period may not be too far off. Remember, these changes are not a race. You might be like Ava and start seeing changes early, or you might be more like Mia and start noticing them a bit later. Both are perfectly normal. Everyone has their unique timeline.

To help manage these changes, here are some things Ava did, which might also help you:

- ★ She started keeping a journal to note any changes or feelings she's experiencing. It helped her understand her body better and also served as a useful tool when she needed to talk about these changes with her mother or doctor.

- ★ Whenever Ava felt uncomfortable with the changes, she practiced deep breathing exercises. She found that taking slow, deep breaths helped her feel calmer and more grounded.

- ★ Ava also found that regular physical activity made her feel healthier and happier, whether it was playing a game of basketball, going for a swim, or simply taking a walk around the block.

Remember, your journey through puberty is unique to you. It's okay to feel excited, confused, or even a bit scared. Just like any adventure, it's filled with new experiences and discoveries. But as you navigate through it, remember that it's your journey, it's your adventure, and you're not alone. You have your friends, family, and this guide to accompany you along the way.

AGE RANGE	CHANGES OCCURRING
8-12	Beginning of breast development
9-14	Pubic hair starts to appear
10-14	Growth spurt in height and weight
11-14	Menstruation begins
12-16	Underarm hair grows
14-18	Fully developed reproductive system

☆ 1.3 EMBRACING INDIVIDUAL DIFFERENCES

Every person is unique, just like every snowflake that falls from the sky. We each have our own special spark that makes us different from everyone else, and that's something to celebrate. As you grow and your body begins to change, you'll notice that not everyone is experiencing the same changes at the same time or in the same way, and that's perfectly okay. In fact, it's quite wonderful! Puberty is a journey that each of us embarks on at our own speed. It's kind of like a giant puzzle. Each piece fits together in its own way to create a unique picture, and each picture is beautiful in its own right. In bodies, for example, these differences are often easily noticeable. Some girls may start growing taller earlier than others. Some may develop curves sooner. And while some may start seeing changes in their skin, like pimples or zits, others may not experience this at all. Imagine that you and your best friend planted two seeds in each of your gardens. Even if you planted them at the same time and cared for them in the same way, those seeds would grow into plants differently. One might sprout leaves first, and the other might shoot up taller first. Just like those seeds, our bodies grow and change in their own unique ways.

Next, there's the mind, which is just as unique as our bodies. We all think differently, feel differently, and see things from our unique viewpoints. Some girls might become more sensitive during puberty, while others might become more outgoing. Some might develop a love for a new hobby or interest, while others might continue enjoying what they've always loved. Puberty is a time of emotional roller-coasters. One minute you might feel on top of the world, and the next, you might feel like everything is crashing down. Some girls may experience these ups and downs more intensely than others. It's important to remember that there is no "normal" or "abnormal" here. It's all part of the journey of growing up. What matters most is accepting yourself for who you are. In the same way, it's vital to respect others for their unique journeys. We might all be different, but in our differences, we are all special.

Let's imagine a day at school. You notice that your friend Olivia has started to wear a bra, while you haven't yet. You might think something like "Oh no, why am I not wearing a bra yet? Does this mean I'm behind?" This is a common thought for girls your age, but remember - everyone develops at their own pace. There is no 'right' or 'wrong' time to start needing a bra. It's simply a matter of when your body decides it's time.

- Exercise I: Write down how you feel when you notice someone developing faster or slower than you. Do you feel anxious, curious, or maybe even a bit jealous? It's okay to have these feelings. Recognize them, write them down, and remind yourself that everyone is different.

Let's take another situation. Your best friend, Mia, has started to get pimples. You feel lucky that you don't have any yet, but you also feel bad for Mia. This is a good moment to practice empathy.

- Exercise 2: At home, stand in front of a mirror and imagine you have a big pimple right in the middle of your forehead. How do you feel? Now, write a supportive message to Mia, understanding her situation and reminding her that it's normal and okay to have pimples during puberty.

Some girls start getting their periods earlier than others. This can lead to various situations, like having to bring a pad or tampon to school, or dealing with cramps.

- Exercise 3: Imagine it's you who got your period first in your class. How would you feel? Would you be proud, scared, or maybe a little of both? Write down your feelings, and then write a list of questions you would have. This will help you be prepared when your time comes and make you empathetic towards friends who start their period before you.

Let's switch gears and think about emotions. During puberty, girls start to experience stronger emotions. Jenny, a girl in your class, has been crying a lot lately. Some kids are making fun of her, but you know it's probably because she's going through puberty.

- Exercise 4: Write a short story about a day in Jenny's life. How does she feel when she wakes up in the morning, goes to school, comes home, and goes to bed? By putting yourself in Jenny's shoes, you can develop empathy and understanding for her situation.

These exercises are meant to help you understand and appreciate the different experiences other girls might be going through during puberty. Remember, we're all different and that's a good thing! It's essential to be patient with yourself and others as we navigate these new changes. And finally, one important thing to remember is to avoid comparing yourself to others or competing with them. We're all on our unique path, and it's not a race to the finish line.

UNIQUE CHARACTERISTICS	HOW TO EMBRACE
Physical Appearance	Appreciate your body and looks
Personality Traits	Understand it is your uniqueness
Mental Abilities	Never compare yourself with others
Emotional Differences	Share and talk about your feelings

Journal Exercise:

Think of your closest friends. Write a short paragraph for each friend that describes the things you think make them unique. It could be about their physical appearance, their talents, or their personality.

Now think about yourself. Write at least three paragraphs describing what makes YOU unique. Consider your physical features, your abilities, and the parts of your personality that you think make you special.

Reflect on how these differences do not make you or your friends better or worse, but instead make you all unique and wonderful in your own way. How does this make you feel about your own individuality? How can you celebrate these differences in yourself and others, instead of comparing or judging?

Chapter 2
PHYSICAL CHANGES AND HEALTH

☆ 2.1 UNDERSTANDING YOUR BODY'S TRANSFORMATION

The changes that come with growing up can often be confusing and even a little scary, but it's all a natural part of life. One of the key periods of your life when you'll experience lots of changes is during puberty. This is your body's way of transforming from a girl into a young woman. Let's explore what these changes are all about. When we talk about puberty, the first thing that usually comes to mind is growth. You might start to notice that your clothes are a bit tighter than they used to be, or that you can now reach things that used to be too high for you. This is what we call a 'growth spurt', where your body grows much faster than it has before. Usually, girls experience this between the ages of 9 and 14, but don't worry if you're a bit earlier or later - everyone is different! Another aspect of this growth is the development of your secondary sexual characteristics, which are physical features that differentiate adult men and women but are not directly related to reproduction. So, what are these characteristics for girls?

☆ Firstly, your hips will start to widen. This is your body preparing for potential future childbirth.

☆ Secondly, your breasts will begin to grow. This is often one of the first noticeable changes in girls going through puberty. It's also important to note that it's very normal for one breast to grow faster than the other at first.

★ The third change you might notice is hair growing in different places such as under your arms and in the pubic area. This is absolutely normal and part of becoming a woman.

★ Another typical change is the start of your menstrual cycle, your period. This is a monthly cycle where your body prepares itself for potential pregnancy.

Remember, all these changes are a perfectly normal part of growing up. Everyone goes through them at their own pace, and there's no 'right' or 'wrong' time for them to happen. The important thing is to understand what's happening and to know that it's all part of the amazing journey of growing up. In the next part, we will delve deeper into practical scenarios and ways to navigate through these changes. Remember that it's okay to feel unsure or even scared about these changes. No one expects you to have all the answers, and there's no shame in asking questions. Change can be daunting, but with the right knowledge and support, it can also be an exciting journey to unfold. Be proud of your body and the transformation it's going through. This is a special time of your life, and it's something to be celebrated.

Journal Exercise:

1. Draw a picture of how you imagine your body will look like after going through puberty. Label the changes you expect to see.

2. Write down three feelings you have about your body's transformation. It could be excitement, anxiety, confusion, or any other feelings you have.

3. Do you think the changes you might go through are normal? If not, why so?

4. Write down two things you learned about puberty from this chapter that you didn't know before.

5. Describe a conversation you might have with a trusted adult (such as a parent, guardian, or teacher) about the changes you are experiencing during puberty.

6. Remember, it's okay to feel a little scared or confused. Puberty is a normal part of growing up and everyone goes through it.

☆ 2.2 THE BASICS OF THE FEMALE REPRODUCTIVE SYSTEM

FEMALE REPRODUCTIVE SYSTEM

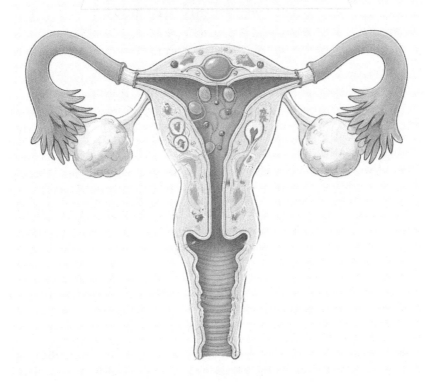

The journey through puberty can be like stepping into a whole new world. Your body starts to change, and you begin to experience feelings and sensing things you might not have before.

One of the key players in this process is your own body's female reproductive system. Let's imagine your body as a beautiful, intricate garden, and at the heart of it is the female reproductive system, lovingly taking care of the flowers of life. It's made up of various parts, each with a unique and important function.

Starting from the outside and working our way in, the first part of the system is the vulva. This is an umbrella term that includes all the external parts that you can see, such as the labia and the clitoris. The labia are like protective petals, while the clitoris is a little bud of sensation, all playing their role in the garden of your body. Inside, you'll find the vagina, a kind of magical, multipurpose tunnel. It's where menstrual blood leaves the body, where babies are born, and it can also be a source of pleasure. Like a gatekeeper, the cervix rests at the top of the vagina, leading to the next part of the system: the uterus. The uterus, or womb, is like a super-special flower bed. Every month, it prepares itself to potentially grow a new life. It does this by lining its walls with a nutrient-rich layer. If a fertilized egg doesn't implant here, this lining sheds, leading to your period. Connected to the uterus are the fallopian tubes, kind of like the watering can of your garden. They transport eggs from the ovaries to the uterus. Speaking of the ovaries, they're like the seeds of life. They store and release eggs, and also produce hormones - estrogen and progesterone - that orchestrate the symphony of puberty.

During puberty, your reproductive system starts to mature, and the garden begins to blossom. Every month, one of your ovaries releases an egg, a process called ovulation. At the same time, your uterus prepares itself for potential pregnancy. If the egg isn't fertilized, the uterus lining sheds and you experience your period. This cycle is called the menstrual cycle and it's one of the most observable signs of puberty. It's a beautiful system, but it can also be a bit of a roller coaster, especially during puberty. Your body is learning how to manage the cycle, and this can lead to irregular periods, mood swings, and other changes. But don't worry! This is a natural part of growing up and becoming an adult.

PART OF THE SYSTEM	DESCRIPTION
Ovaries	These are where eggs are stored and hormonal production takes place.
Fallopian Tubes	These are pathways for eggs to travel from the ovaries to the uterus.
Uterus	This is the location where an embryo develops into a fetus.
Cervix	This is the passage connecting the uterus to the vagina.
Vagina	Also known as the birth canal
Labia and Clitoris	These parts are involved in sexual response and sensation.

Journal Exercise:

1. Draw a simple diagram of the female reproductive system as explained in the chapter. Label each part and write a brief description of what its function is.

2. How did you feel when you were reading about the changes your body will go through? Write down any feelings or thoughts you had. Remember, it's perfectly normal to feel a mix of emotions about growing up!

3. Based on what you read, what do you think is the most surprising thing about the female reproductive

system? What did you already know, and what was new information?

4. Imagine you have a younger sister or friend who is curious about puberty. How would you explain the female reproductive system to her using your own words?

5. Reflect on the importance of understanding your own body as you go through puberty. How do you think knowing more about your reproductive system can help you during this phase of your life?

☆ 2.3 THE STAGES OF BREAST DEVELOPMENT

As you approach puberty, one of the changes you may notice is in your chest area, and it's all part of a normal process called breast development. This happens in stages, and each one brings unique changes to your body. It all starts with the flat stage, often known as stage one. This is where you are before puberty begins. Your chest might look the same as it did when you were a little kid, but changes are on the horizon. Enter puberty and stage two. This is when the first visible signs of growth appear. You might notice small, slightly raised bumps, usually around the age of 8 to 13. These are breast buds, the very beginnings of what will eventually become your breasts. During this time, your chest might feel a bit tender or sore. This is normal, and a sign that your body is preparing for the stages to come. In stage three, your breasts start to grow a little more. They become rounder and fuller, and your areolas (the darker area surrounding your nipples) might expand. This stage often happens when you're between the ages of 12 and 14. Next comes stage four. Not only do your breasts continue to grow, but also the shape starts to change. They might become more oval or maintain a more rounded shape. Regardless, the most notable change is that your nipples and areolas start to protrude. This is often seen in girls between the ages of 13 and 15. Finally, we arrive at stage five, the final stage of breast development. This is when your breasts reach their adult size and shape. The nipples and areolas also form a separate contour from the rest of the breast. This stage usually happens when you're between the ages of 15 and 18, but remember everyone's body is different, so it may come sooner or later.

Now, here's something to keep in mind: timelines for these stages are estimates and it's completely normal if you experience these changes earlier or later than the typical age ranges. Everybody develops at their own pace, and your body knows when it's the right time for you to grow. Rest assured, these changes are all part of becoming the person you're meant to be. Also, each of your breasts might not grow at the same rate. In other words, one might be a little bigger than the other. This is normal too, and over time, they usually even out. But even if they don't, that's perfectly okay. Every body is unique and beautiful in its own way.

STAGE	DESCRIPTION
Pre-teen	Flatten chest area with only small bumps known as breast buds.
Early Teen	Breast buds start to grow bigger
Mid Teen	Breasts and nipples continue to grow and become round
Late Teen	Breasts fully developed
Adult	Final size and shape of breasts reached

Let's take a real-life scenario to understand this better. Let's think about Jessica. Jessica is 9 years old and she's noticed some changes happening to her body. She's beginning to grow breasts and she's not sure what to make of it.

Jessica noticed that her chest area was a little bit tender. She was at home, trying on her usual t-shirt, and it felt a bit snug. She looked at herself in the mirror, and there was a small bump – almost like a small hill. So, she went to her mom and they talked about it. This stage, where the small bump appears, is often referred to as the ‚budding stage' or Stage 2 of breast development. Jessica's mom explained this to her and assured her that it's completely normal.

1. As months passed, Jessica noticed more changes. The small hill under her shirt started growing a bit bigger. Jessica felt a bit self-conscious about it, especially when she was playing sports. It was the Stage 3 of breast development. Jessica's mom showed her how to wear a sports bra which could provide her with comfort and support during her physical activities.

2. By the time Jessica turned II, the small hill had grown into a mound – the full breast shape wasn't there but it was more than a bump now. It was Stage 4. Jessica's mom helped her to buy her first training bra. Jessica felt a bit more confident knowing that she was going through changes just like all her friends.

3. Gradually, Jessica's breasts continued to develop and by the age of 14, she had fully developed breasts – Stage 5. She had learned about how to care for them and understood the importance of wearing the right size and type of bra.

Now let's talk about some misconceptions:

☆ The first one that Jessica had was that all girls develop at the same pace. She noticed some of her friends were developing faster than her, and it worried her. But Jessica's mother explained that every girl's body is unique and develops at its own pace.

★ Another misconception Jessica had was that both breasts are supposed to be the exact same size. Her mother told her that it is normal for one breast to be slightly larger than the other. Symmetry is not a rule when it comes to bodies!

★ Jessica also thought that she might be sick because her breasts were tender. But, that tenderness was a normal part of the development process. Her mom taught her how to do a self-examination of her breasts to ensure they're healthy.

You can take away a few things from Jessica's journey:

★ It's normal to feel unsure and have lots of questions. Talking to a trusted adult can really help.

★ It's important to know that everyone's body is unique and develops at its own pace.

★ It's also crucial to learn how to choose the right type of bra for your comfort and support, especially while playing sports.

★ Self-examinations are a good way to keep track of your health.

Remember, it's okay to have questions and doubts. Growing up isn't easy, but with the right guidance, you can navigate it with grace and confidence. Your body is your own, and it's important to understand it and take care of it. The journey from being a girl to a young woman is special, and these changes are a part of that incredible journey.

Journal Exercise:

1. Describe in your own words what happens during the different stages of breast development.

2. How did it make you feel reading about these changes? Do you feel more aware and prepared or does it still seem a little scary?

3. Draw a line on a piece of paper from 1 to 10 to represent a 'confidence scale'. At 1, it would mean you're 'Not confident at all', at 10 you're 'Extremely confident'. Mark on the scale where you think you lie in terms of understanding how your body will change during puberty.

4. What questions do you still have about breast development? If there are any, write them down. It's perfectly normal to have questions and it's an important part of the learning process.

5. Write a short paragraph about how you hope to handle these changes. This can include practical things like buying new clothes, but also your emotional approach. Remember, there's no right or wrong answer - this is all about your feelings and thoughts.

☆ 2.4 DEALING WITH NEW BODY HAIR AND SKINCARE TIPS

Have you spotted a few extra strands of hair on your body lately, perhaps on your arms, legs, or underarms? Don't be alarmed, this is a completely normal part of growing up. As you inch closer to your teens, your body begins to undergo several changes, one of which is the growth of new body hair. Let's understand why this happens. Your body produces hormones, special chemicals that tell different parts of your body what to do. Around the time of puberty, your body begins to produce more of a hormone called androgen. Androgens are often referred to as male hormones, but they're produced in both boys and girls during puberty, and they're responsible for the growth of new hair on different parts of your body.

Now, where does this hair start to appear? Some of the most common spots include the underarms, the pubic area (that's the area between your legs), and the legs. Some girls also notice more hair on their arms or even a little on their upper lip. This new hair might feel a little strange at first. It can be darker and thicker than the hair on your head, but that's nothing to worry about. It's all part of becoming a teenager.

So, how do you care for this new hair? Here are a few pointers:

☆ Keep it clean: Just like the hair on your head, the new hair on your body needs to be washed regularly with warm water and mild soap. This helps keep your skin clear and prevents unpleasant body odor.

☆ Be gentle: While it might be tempting to scrub at this new hair to try and remove it, resist the urge. Your skin around these areas can be sensitive, and harsh scrubbing can cause irritation.

☆ Keep it dry: After you bathe, make sure you dry these areas thoroughly. Dampness can lead to skin irritations and infections.

☆ Wear comfortable clothes: Tight clothing can cause sweating and friction, which can irritate your skin. Opt for clothes made from natural fibers like cotton, which allow your skin to breathe.

Remember, everybody develops at their own pace, so you might notice new hair before or after your friends do. That's perfectly okay and it's nothing to worry about. The most important thing is to stay clean and comfortable as you navigate this new aspect of growing up.

Taking a glance at your skin, you may notice it's not the same as it used to be. This is completely okay and part of your journey into becoming a young woman. As we've learned, new body hair is a normal part of puberty. However, it's equally important to focus on skincare. Having a proper skincare routine is not just about looking good, but it's also about feeling good and keeping your skin healthy. Let's imagine a young girl named Olivia. She's just entered puberty and is dealing with oily skin, a common problem during this time. Olivia has made up her mind to take care of her skin, and so, we'll help her create a skincare routine suitable for her teenage skin.

The first step in Olivia's routine is cleansing. It's important to wash your face twice a day — once in the morning and once before bed. For Olivia, who has oily skin, a gel-based cleanser would work best. These types of cleansers are designed to deep clean the pores, removing excess oil and dirt without stripping the face of its natural oils.

1. Once Olivia has cleaned her face, the next step is toning. A good toner will help remove any leftover dirt or makeup, balance the skin's pH level, and also help control oil production.

2. The final step in the routine is moisturization. Even though Olivia has oily skin, it's important that she doesn't skip this step. Depriving the skin of moisture will only cause it to produce more oil. For someone with oily skin, a lightweight or oil-free moisturizer would work best.

3. Exercise: You can create your own skincare routine following these steps. Keep in mind that everybody's skin is different and what works for Olivia might not work for you. Try different products until you find what suits your skin best.

Remember, it's okay and perfectly normal to experience skin problems during puberty. Common issues include acne, blackheads, and oily skin. Most of these problems are due to hormonal changes and will resolve over time. But, in case you're dealing with severe acne or other skin issues, don't hesitate to consult a dermatologist.

When it comes to dealing with new body hair, let's imagine another situation. One day, Olivia noticed some hair under her arms while changing for PE class. She felt a little embarrassed and wasn't sure what to do. If you find yourself in a similar situation, remember that this is a normal part of growing up. One way to handle new body hair could be talking to an adult you trust about it. When Olivia talked to her mom, she felt better knowing that she wasn't alone and that it's something all girls go through. Her mom explained that she could choose to leave the hair as it is or remove it if she wants. Some girls choose to shave, some wax, and others use hair removal creams.

Exercise: If you're not sure how you feel about your new body hair yet, that's okay. You can take some time to think about it. You can also try writing about how you feel in a journal. Remember, the decision of what to do with your new body hair is entirely up to you.

Journal Exercise:

1. Write about your feelings when you first noticed new hair growing on different parts of your body. Were you surprised, excited, scared or confused? Explain why you felt that way.

2. List three new changes you've noticed about your skin. Have you been able to manage these changes effectively? Explain how.

3. What have you learnt about taking care of your skin from the chapter? List down three skincare tips that you found most helpful.

4. How has the information in the chapter helped ease your worries about new body hair and skin changes? Write a short paragraph on this using your own words.

☆ 2.5 GROWTH SPURTS: CHANGES IN HEIGHT AND WEIGHT

Growth spurts! It's a term you might've heard tossed around, especially when talking about teens. But what exactly are they, and how do they relate to changes in your height and weight? Let's delve into this intriguing topic, shall we? Simply put, a growth spurt is a period of rapid growth in height and weight. It's like a quick zoom ahead on the road of growth. During puberty, your body undergoes several growth spurts, although the exact number and timing can vary for everyone.

To begin with, let's picture our bodies like a building. Buildings aren't constructed overnight, and they follow a blueprint. Similarly, our bodies have a blueprint in the form of DNA, and growth is a gradual process. However, during puberty—our body's construction boom—the speed of this process picks up dramatically! Height is one of the most noticeable changes during a growth spurt. You might suddenly find yourself towering over your classmates, or perhaps you notice your friends outgrowing you. This rapid increase in height happens due to the growth of bones, particularly the long ones in your legs and arms.

But along with height, weight also changes during a growth spurt. As your body grows taller, it also needs to fill out and develop a balanced shape. So, you'll likely notice an increase in your overall body mass. This can include everything from your muscles to your organs, and yes, even a little bit of fat, which is perfectly normal! It can be a bit surprising, almost like your body is a stranger. One day your favorite pair of jeans fit perfectly, the next day they're feeling a bit tight or too short. This, dear reader, is the magic (and sometimes the trickery) of growth spurts. While the way each person experiences growth spurts can be different, there are a few common signs:

★ Outgrowing clothes or shoes quickly

★ A sudden increase in appetite

★ Feeling tired more often

Imagine this: it's the first day of summer vacation and you've just pulled out your favorite pair of shorts from last year, but when you try to put them on, they're too small. Or maybe you've noticed that you're suddenly taller than your best friend, even though you were the same height just a few months ago. These are classic examples of growth spurts in action.

Let's take a look at how you can navigate these changes with ease, confidence, and balance.

The first thing to remember is that every girl's body is unique. Some might grow tall quickly, others more slowly, and that's okay. Here's a little story about a girl named Lily to illustrate this point. Lily was the shortest girl in her 4th grade class. One summer, she had a big growth spurt and when she returned to school, she was suddenly one of the tallest. At first, Lily felt uncomfortable with her new height and was worried about what the other kids would say. But instead of letting these worries get her down, Lily found ways to embrace her new height. She loved playing basketball and realized her height gave her an advantage on the court. So, she decided to join a local team and soon found herself enjoying her new height and the confidence that came with it. In Lily's case, finding an activity that made her feel good about her changing body helped her navigate her growth spurt. You can do the same by finding activities that you love, which make you feel confident and happy with your body, whether it's a sport, dance, yoga, or simply going for walks in the park.

Now, growth spurts can also affect your weight, and this is not something to shy away from. Let's consider another story of a girl named Mia. Mia had always been quite slim but during a growth spurt, she noticed that she had put on some weight. At first, she felt self-conscious about these changes, especially since some of her clothes didn't fit as they used to. But instead of worrying, Mia took it upon herself to learn more about balanced nutrition. She discovered that during growth spurts, it's normal for the body's demand for nutrients to increase. That's why she was feeling hungry more often. So, Mia started paying more attention to what she ate. She included more fruits, vegetables, lean proteins, and whole grains in her meals. She also made sure to drink plenty of water and limited the amount of sugary drinks and snacks.

Here are a few nutrition tips Mia followed that you can use too:

1. Make half of your plate fruits and vegetables: They provide essential vitamins and minerals that your body needs to grow and stay healthy.

2. Include protein in each meal: Proteins are the building blocks of your body, essential for growth and repair.

3. Choose whole grains: They provide energy and make you feel fuller for longer.

4. Stay hydrated: Drink water throughout the day to keep your body functioning at its best.

So, if you notice changes in your weight during a growth spurt, remember Mia's story. Learn about balanced nutrition and make healthy food choices. And remember, it's perfectly okay to indulge in your favorite treat once in a while!

Journal Exercise:

1. Record your current height and weight (don't worry, this journal is for your eyes only!). Are you tall, short, average? Do these labels matter? Why or why not?

2. Growth spurts can lead to "growing pains." Have you experienced any discomfort or aches as you've grown? How do you deal with these feelings?

3. Write about a moment when you realized you were growing up because you had grown physically. How did it impact your perception of yourself?

4. Reflect on your personal relationship with food and exercise. How have they contributed to your growth and overall health? Can you make a promise to yourself to keep a balanced perspective on this in the future?

5. Changes during growth spurts are natural and different for everyone. How have the experiences shared in the chapter made you feel about your own growth and development?

☆ 2.6 PERSONAL HYGIENE: CARING FOR YOUR CHANGING BODY

Wonderful things happen when a girl grows up. It's like being the heroine of your own story where every chapter brings something new and exciting. The exciting thing about these changes is that they're a sign that you're growing up. It's like your body saying, "Hey, I'm getting ready for some pretty amazing things in the future!" But with these exciting developments, also comes the need for a little extra care. This is where personal hygiene comes in. In the simplest terms, personal hygiene is the practice of keeping your body clean to prevent illness and enhance your overall well-being. This might mean taking a shower or bath regularly, washing your hands, brushing your teeth, and using deodorant. When you step into puberty, your body's increased production of hormones can lead to more sweat and oil production. But don't worry, these changes are perfectly normal, and there are plenty of ways to take care of them. Just think of it as adding a few extra steps in your daily routine.

Let's look at some specific ways you can take care of your changing body during puberty. These practical habits can make your adventure into womanhood smoother and more comfortable. Let's start this journey with a scenario. Imagine waking up one bright and sunny morning. The birds are chirping, the sky is blue, and you're excited about a fun day planned with friends. As you sit up and stretch, you suddenly notice a strange, unfamiliar smell. It's sort of... well, funky. Quickly, you realize it's you! You're dealing with some body odor, a common occurrence during puberty. Here's what you can do:

☆ Shower Regularly: Start your day with a refreshing shower, using a mild soap and warm water. Pay extra attention to areas prone to sweat such as armpits and feet. Showering removes sweat and bacteria, preventing body odor.

☆ Wear Clean Clothes: Make sure your clothes, especially underwear and socks, are clean and fresh. Sweat can cling to fabrics, creating an environment where bacteria thrive and cause odor.

☆ Use Deodorant: Once you start experiencing body odor, it might be time to consider using deodorant. Choose a gentle one designed for sensitive skin. Remember, it's totally normal to need deodorant at this stage, and it's nothing to be embarrassed about!

Next, let's talk about hair care. Your hair might start to get oilier during puberty due to increased hormone levels. Here's how you can manage it:

★ Wash Your Hair Often: Depending on how oily your hair gets, you may need to wash it every day or every other day. Use a mild shampoo and focus on cleaning the scalp rather than the ends of your hair.

★ Brush Regularly: Brushing your hair not only detangles it but also helps distribute the natural oils from your scalp to the ends of your hair. This can make your hair look shinier and healthier!

Now, onto dental hygiene. During puberty, your body is changing, and that includes your mouth too! You might notice that your breath isn't quite as fresh as it used to be, or your gums might be a bit more sensitive. Here's how to keep your oral hygiene on track:

★ Brush Twice a Day: Brush your teeth every morning and every night before bed. Use a soft-bristled toothbrush and fluoride toothpaste. Brush for at least two minutes, cleaning all surfaces of your teeth.

★ Floss Daily: Flossing removes plaque and food particles from between your teeth where your toothbrush can't reach. If you find flossing difficult, a water flosser could be an easier option.

★ Visit the Dentist Regularly: Try to visit your dentist every six months for a check-up and professional cleaning. They can spot any potential issues early and give you advice tailored to your specific needs.

Lastly, let's talk about skincare. Puberty can bring about various skin changes, like acne. Here's how to maintain clear skin:

★ Keep Your Face Clean: Wash your face twice a day with a gentle cleanser. Never go to bed with makeup on - it can clog your pores and cause breakouts.

★ Moisturize: Even if your skin seems oilier, it still needs moisture! Look for a lightweight, oil-free moisturizer to keep your skin healthy without adding extra oil.

★ Be Gentle: If you do get a pimple, resist the urge to pick or squeeze it. This can lead to scarring and more breakouts. Instead, apply a spot treatment with salicylic acid or benzoyl peroxide and let it heal naturally.

Remember, everyone goes through these changes during puberty. It's a normal part of growing up, so there's nothing to be embarrassed about.

Journal Exercise:

1. Think about your current daily hygiene routine. Do you think the new information you learned will cause you to change it? If so, sketch out what your new routine might look like.

2. Describe what you understand about the importance of personal cleanliness as you grow up. How did this chapter help you understand its significance?

Chapter 3
MENSTRUATION AND YOU

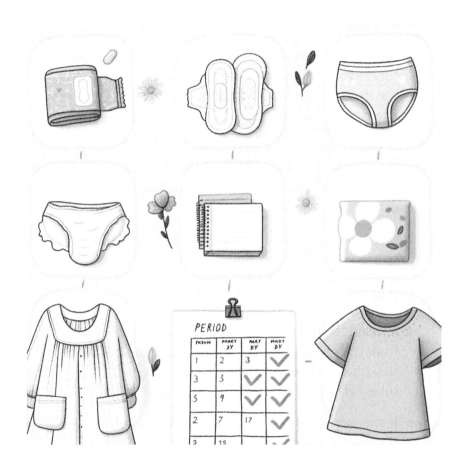

☆ 3.1 DEMYSTIFYING MENSTRUATION

Take a moment and imagine your body like a beautiful, complex tree. Each part, from the roots to the highest leaves, has its own special purpose. Your body as a girl, too, is an amazing creation with many intricate processes happening all the time. One such vital process you will experience as you grow is menstruation. This might sound like a big, unfamiliar word right now, but by the end of this, you'll understand it just fine. The process of menstruation is part of a larger cycle called the menstrual cycle. This cycle is like a dance that your body performs every month, and menstruation is one part of that dance. To simplify it, let's break it down:

★ Your menstrual cycle begins with your pituitary gland. This tiny organ at the base of your brain is like the director of the dance. It sends out signals or hormones to your ovaries - two almond-shaped organs in your lower belly.

★ These hormones tell the ovaries to start maturing an egg. It's like the ovary is a nest and the egg has to grow before it's ready to fly. This process takes about two weeks and is called the follicular phase.

★ Meanwhile, another hormone tells the lining of your uterus or womb to start thickening. This lining is like a soft, comfy cushion, preparing in case the mature egg needs a place to land.

★ Around the middle of the cycle, the mature egg is released from the ovary in what's called ovulation. It's like the egg has spread its wings and is ready to fly. It travels down a tube called the fallopian tube towards the uterus.

★ If the egg is not fertilized by a sperm, it doesn't attach to the uterus. The comfy cushion lining is not needed, so your body sheds it. This shedding is what we call menstruation or a period. The process starts all over again with another egg in the ovary, and the cycle continues.

Now, you might be wondering, why does this happen? Well, this cycle is your body's natural way of preparing for a potential pregnancy. It's like your body is practicing for something it might need to do in the future. It's an essential part of feminine puberty and a sign your body is maturing and growing. Remember, your body is like a wonderful, complex tree. The process of menstruation is a part of your growth, like a tree spreading its roots, growing taller, and flowering. It's nothing to fear, but rather, a fascinating dance your body performs each month. It's a dance of life, a celebration of growing up, and a part of becoming the amazing woman you're destined to be.

Journal Exercise:

Write a brief letter to your future self about how you see and understand menstruation now, after reading this chapter. Include your feelings about getting your first period. Share any worries or fears you may have and also any questions that you still need answers to. You may want to include things you want to remember or advice you want to give to your future self. Remember this is a healthy and natural part of growing up, and it's okay to express all feelings, whether they are positive, negative, or mixed.

☆ 3.2 PREPARING FOR YOUR FIRST PERIOD

You're about to embark on a new journey, and just like any well-prepared explorer, you need to pack the essentials. Your Period Kit will become your trusty sidekick, always ready in your backpack or locker. So, let's dive in and make sure you've got everything you need for when your period decides to make its grand entrance.

Crafting Your Ultimate Period Kit:

Your Period Kit is your first-aid kit for period days. It's personal, so you can make it as simple or as fancy as you like. Here's a detailed guide on how to create one:

- ★ Pads: These are your first line of defense. There are all sorts of pads, from ultra-thins to overnights, with wings or without. Wings are like little flaps that fold over the sides of your underwear to keep the pad in place and offer extra protection. You might want to start with a variety pack to see which ones you prefer. Try them on with different types of underwear to see which combo feels best. Remember to change your pad every 4 to 6 hours, or more often if it's full and feels uncomfortable.

- ★ Spare Underwear: Choose a comfortable pair, maybe not your favorite unicorn ones, but something you won't mind having as a backup. Dark colors are a great choice because they're less likely to show any stains. Roll them up tight so they don't take much space in your kit.

- ★ Wipes: These can be simple baby wipes or special feminine hygiene wipes that are gentle on your skin. They're perfect for helping you feel clean and fresh if you're not able to take a shower right away. You can get individually wrapped ones to keep them clean and discreet in your kit.

- ★ A Ziplock Bag: This is for those just-in-case moments. If you have a leak and need to change, you can put your used underwear in this bag and seal it up until you get home. No mess, no stress!

- ★ Pain Reliever: Sometimes periods can bring along aches called cramps. Talk to your parent or guardian about including a pain reliever like ibuprofen or acetaminophen. They can show you the correct dose to take and when. Remember, you should never share medication or take anyone else's. Keep it in its original, labeled bottle to avoid any mix-ups.

Extra Comforts:

Here are a few other things you might want to include in your kit for those days when you need a little extra TLC:

- ★ A Small Heat Pad or Hot Water Bottle: These can be a lifesaver if you have cramps. You won't be able to use them in class, but as soon as you're home, they can be very comforting.

- ★ Chocolate or a Small Snack: Sometimes a little sugar can boost your mood. Plus, it's a nice treat to look forward to!

- ★ A Note of Encouragement: Write yourself a little note or ask someone you love to write one for you. It can be a simple „You've got this!" or a reminder of how strong and amazing you are.

ITEM	DESCRIPTION
Pads	Variety pack (ultra-thins, overnights, with/ without wings). Change every 4-6 hours or as needed.
Spare Underwear	Comfortable pair, preferably dark colored. Roll up tightly for compact storage.
Wipes	Baby wipes or feminine hygiene wipes. Individually wrapped for cleanliness and discretion.
Ziplock Bag	For storing used underwear discreetly in case of leaks. Seals to prevent mess.

ITEM	DESCRIPTION
Pain Reliever	Ibuprofen or acetaminophen. Consult with a guardian for correct dosage. Keep in original labeled bottle.
Small Heat Pad or Hot Water Bottle	Useful for comforting cramps at home. Not for use in class.
Chocolate or a Small Snack	A little sugar can boost your mood. Keep a small, enjoyable treat in your kit.
Note of Encouragement	A personal or written note for encouragement. A reminder of your strength and resilience.

Practice Time:

Now, let's talk practice. You might be thinking, "Why would I wear a pad if I don't have my period yet?" Great question! Practicing lets you get used to how it feels to wear a pad. You can move around, jump, sit, stand, and find out that you can do everything you normally do, even with a pad. It's like a dress rehearsal for the real show. Select a day when you're just hanging out at home. Put on the pad, and wear it for a few hours. You'll see how it fits and feels, and you can practice changing it too. This way, when your period does come, you'll be a pad-changing pro!

Dress Rehearsal - Outfit Planning:

When it comes to what to wear during your period, comfort is key. Start thinking about your "period-friendly" wardrobe now. It doesn't mean you have to give up on style—just think about what might make you feel more at ease. Maybe it's pants with a bit more room, leggings with a long sweater, or dresses with dark patterns. The goal is to find outfits that make you feel confident and worry-free about leaks. Try this fun activity: Have a fashion show at home with your potential period outfits. It's a good way to see which clothes make you feel secure and comfy. Plus, it's an excellent excuse to strut your stuff down the runway of your hallway!

Understanding Your Body's Signals:

Your body is amazing and will send you little messages to let you know that your period could be starting soon. You might feel a bit bloated, like your belly is full of air, or you could have some achy feelings in your lower back or tummy. Some girls also feel extra tired or moody. If you start to notice these signs, it's a good idea to start carrying your Period Kit with you. Keep a little diary of how you feel each day. You might start to see a pattern and be able to predict when your period is coming. This is like becoming a detective for your own body, and the clues can really help you out!

Calendars and Apps - Your Secret Weapon

Marking down the start and end of your period each month is super helpful. You can use a regular wall calendar or a special period tracker app. These apps are cool because they can predict when your next period might come, and they're usually password-protected, so your info is private. Every time your period starts, put a big dot or sticker on that day. Pretty soon, you'll be able to see if your period is regular—like clockwork, or a little unpredictable, which is totally normal too.

Having a Plan - School and Home Strategies:

Let's strategize for when you're at school:

> ★ Where to Go: Know which bathrooms are the most private and where you can take a few extra minutes if you need to.

★ Buddy System: Have a friend who knows about your Period Kit. If you forget yours, they might have supplies to share.

★ Teacher Trust: Identify a teacher or school nurse you can trust. If you feel unwell or need to go to the bathroom outside of the usual times, they'll understand why.

And for home:

★ Supply Station: Decide where you'll keep your supplies. A bathroom drawer? A special box in your room?

★ Family Code: Come up with a code word with your family. That way, if you need to say you've started your period without announcing it to everyone, you can use your code word.

Let's Talk - The Importance of Communication:

Choosing your Period Buddy is like choosing a teammate. This person should be someone you trust and can talk to about anything, like a parent, older sibling, or family friend. They can help you restock your kit, remind you how normal and natural periods are, and give you a hug when you need one. Remember to check in with your Period Buddy regularly. As you get more used to having your period, you might have new questions or need different supplies. They're there to support you every step of the way.

Preparing for your first period is like preparing for any big moment in life. It's about knowing what to expect, having the right tools, and knowing who to turn to for support. With your detailed Period Kit, a wardrobe that makes you feel unstoppable, a body signals diary, and a solid plan, you'll be more than ready. You'll be in control, confident, and most importantly, you'll still be the amazing you. And remember, you're never alone in this. You're part of a community of millions of girls who are experiencing the same thing. So pack that Period Kit, mark your calendar, and wear your favorite outfit with pride. You're about to join the Period Club, and we're so excited to have you. You're doing great, and if you ever need more advice or have more questions, just ask. We're here for you! Now, how about we get that Period Kit ready?

Journal Exercise:

1. Identify three people you feel comfortable discussing your period with. Why did you choose these people?

2. Imagine you've just started your first period. Write a short, encouraging note to yourself.

3. Reflect on the preparation strategies discussed in this chapter. Which ones do you think will be most helpful for you and why?

☆ 3.3 NAVIGATING PERIOD CHALLENGES

The menstrual cycle comes with its own set of challenges that you may need to navigate. One of the first things you might notice is a physical discomfort. This can vary from girl to girl, but the most common is a kind of cramp or ache in the lower abdomen. This is caused by your uterus contracting to shed its lining, which is what your period is. Some girls also experience things like headaches or a feeling of bloatedness. Let's talk about how you can manage pain during your period. Here's a simple technique you can use to manage pain:

☆ Deep Breathing Exercise: Getting in control of your breath can be an incredible way to manage your pain. Find a quiet and comfortable spot to sit or lie down. Close your eyes and take a slow, deep breath in through your nose. Count to four slowly as you breathe in, then hold your breath for a count of four. Finally, exhale slowly through your mouth for a count of eight. Repeat this cycle for a few minutes and you might find your pain significantly reduced.

Now, let's move on to mood swings, another challenge that can come with periods due to hormonal changes. It's completely normal to feel emotional or upset during this time, but there are ways to keep your mood regulated.

★ Mood Journal: Keeping a mood journal can be very helpful. Each day, make a note of how you're feeling. Write down any emotions you're experiencing and any events that may have triggered these feelings. You might start to notice patterns and identify triggers. This will help you better understand your emotions and manage them.

Finally, maintaining good hygiene during your periods is extremely important. You might be using pads, tampons, or menstrual cups for the first time, and it can seem overwhelming. But don't worry, with a little practice, you'll get the hang of it. Let's look at a specific example of using a menstrual pad:

1. First, unwrap the pad from its packaging. You'll notice that one side of the pad is covered with a peel-off sticker.

2. Remove your underwear and sit or stand in a comfortable position. Peel the sticker off the back of the pad.

3. Stick the pad to the inside of your underwear, making sure it's centered. The sticky side should be stuck to your underwear, and the soft cotton side should be facing up.

4. Adjust the pad until it feels comfortable and secure. Some pads also have wings, which wrap around the sides of your underwear to prevent leaks. If your pad has wings, fold them around the sides of your underwear.

Remember to change your pad at least every 4-6 hours, or sooner if it feels full or uncomfortable. Dispose of the used pad in a bin, not in the toilet.

These are just a few examples and tips to help you navigate the challenges of your period. Remember, everyone's body is different, so what works for one person may not work for you. It's all about finding what helps you feel comfortable and confident during your period.

Journal Exercise:

1. List some concerns or worries you have about periods. Now, after reading this chapter, write down some solutions or comforting facts you've learned that address these worries.

2. Imagine a best friend is nervous about getting her period. Using knowledge from this chapter, write down what advice you would give her to help her navigate this challenge.

☆ 3.4 QUESTIONS AND ANSWERS ABOUT PERIODS

Welcome to the chapter where no question is too small, too weird, or too embarrassing. Periods come with a lot of new experiences and, of course, lots of questions! Here are some real questions that girls just like you have asked, along with some honest and clear answers.

How much blood will I lose during my period?

It might look like a lot, but it's actually not that much. Most girls lose about 2-3 tablespoons of blood during their whole period. That's about the same as the little containers of ketchup you'd get at a fast-food restaurant. If you're ever worried it's too much, talk to your Period Buddy or see a doctor just to be sure.

Will it hurt when I get my period?

Some girls feel a little discomfort or cramping when they get their period, kind of like a stomachache in your lower belly. It's totally normal and usually can be helped with a warm bath, a hot water bottle, or over-the-counter pain relief. If the pain is really bad or stops you from doing things you love, you should talk to a doctor.

How often should I change my pad or tampon?

It's best to change your pad every 4 to 6 hours, even if it's not completely soaked. This helps keep things fresh and prevents any odor. If you use tampons, it's very important to change them every 4 to 6 hours to avoid a rare but serious condition called Toxic Shock Syndrome (TSS). Always use the lowest absorbency tampon you can, and alternate with pads when possible.

Can I still play sports or swim when I have my period?

Absolutely! Your period shouldn't stop you from doing the things you enjoy. For swimming, you might want to use a tampon or a menstrual cup, since pads can absorb water and won't be effective. If you're playing sports, wearing a pad or tampon is totally fine. Just make sure to have extras in your Period Kit in case you need to change.

What if I get my period at school and I'm not prepared?

This happens to the best of us! First, stay calm. You can ask a teacher, school nurse, or a friend if they have supplies. Most schools have pads available for just this situation. Keep a sweater or hoodie in your locker so you can tie it around your waist if you need to cover up. And remember, it's a natural thing that happens to half the population!

Can anyone tell when I'm on my period?

Nope! Your period is your private business. There's no sign that tells everyone you're on your period. If you're worried about leaks, plan your outfit for added security, like wearing dark pants and carrying your Period Kit.

Why do I feel so moody when I get my period?

It's all thanks to hormones, the natural chemicals in your body that get a little wild during your period. They can make you feel like you're on an emotional rollercoaster. It's okay to feel this way. Talking about it, getting some exercise, or doing something you love can help lift your mood.

Do I have to use tampons?

Not at all. It's totally up to you and what you're comfortable with. Pads, tampons, and menstrual cups are all options, and you can try each one to see which works best for you. Some girls start with pads because they're easy to use and then try tampons or menstrual cups later on.

What is PMS?

PMS stands for premenstrual syndrome. It's a bunch of symptoms like bloating, headaches, mood swings, and tiredness that can happen before your period starts. Not everyone gets PMS, and for those who do, the symptoms can vary. Eating well, getting enough sleep, and exercising can help ease PMS symptoms.

These are just a few of the questions you might have, and it's great to ask as many as you need to feel comfortable and confident about your period. Always keep the lines of communication open with your Period Buddy, and never be afraid to seek advice from a trusted adult or healthcare provider. Your questions are important, and getting answers helps you take control of your health and your body. Keep asking, keep learning, and keep being the amazing girl you are!

Chapter 4
EMOTIONAL EVOLUTION

☆ 4.1 UNDERSTANDING MOOD SWINGS

It's super exciting to grow up, isn't it? With all the new experiences, challenges, and changes, it's like you're on one big adventure. But the journey to becoming a teenager isn't always smooth sailing. Sometimes, you might notice that your moods are like a roller coaster: one moment you're on top of the world, the next, you could be feeling low. These emotional ups and downs are called mood swings and they're totally normal during puberty. During puberty, your brain releases a truckload of hormones to help your body grow and mature. Two of the key players in this hormone game are estrogen and progesterone. These are produced in larger quantities during puberty and they're super important because they help in developing your reproductive system, growing breasts, and starting your periods. However, they can also affect your emotions and how you feel. One minute you might feel like laughing with your friends, and the next, you might feel like crying over a sad movie scene. This is because these hormones can influence the chemicals in your brain that regulate mood. When these hormone levels change, they can cause the levels of these chemicals to fluctuate too, leading to mood swings.

You might also notice that your moods can change more frequently around the time of your period. This is because your hormone levels naturally rise and fall during your menstrual cycle. As your body adjusts to these changes, you might feel a bit more emotional or upset than usual. We all go through mood swings from time to time, and it's completely normal. Let's imagine that you're at school, and everything seems perfectly fine in the morning. You're laughing with your friends, acing your math test, and the sun is shining. Suddenly, out of nowhere, you feel a wave of sadness or anger, and you can't figure out why. Does this sound familiar? It's a common example of what a mood swing might look like. Here are some ways to manage these unexpected shifts:

☆ Practice Mindfulness: When a mood swing hits, it can be helpful to practice mindfulness. Take a deep breath, close your eyes, and focus on your breathing. This helps you stay present and makes it a bit easier to handle the mood swing.

★ Journaling: Keeping a mood diary can be really helpful in understanding your mood swings. Note down what happened before the mood swing, how you felt, and what you did to cope with it. After a while, you might notice patterns that can help you prepare for mood swings in the future.

★ Speak Up: Talk to your friends, family, or a trusted adult about your feelings. Sometimes, just saying out loud how you're feeling can make you feel better.

★ Engage in Physical Activity: Regular physical activity can do wonders for your mood. It can help you to release stress and pent-up feelings. If you feel a mood swing coming on, try going for a run or dancing to your favorite song.

Now, let's discuss some exercises that can help develop emotional balance:

1. Deep Breathing: When you feel a mood swing coming on, try a deep breathing exercise. Sit comfortably, close your eyes, and inhale deeply through your nose. Hold your breath for a few seconds, and then slowly exhale through your mouth. Repeat this five times. You may find that your mood swing dissipates or becomes easier to handle.

2. Visualization: This is a calming exercise that can help when you're feeling upset or angry. Close your eyes and imagine a place where you feel completely at peace. It could be a sunny beach, a peaceful forest, or your favorite park. Try to incorporate as many senses as you can: smell the sea air, hear the birds singing, feel the sun on your skin. Stay in your peaceful place for a few minutes, and you might find that your mood has improved.

3. Progressive Muscle Relaxation: This exercise helps you to release physical tension, which can also improve your mood. Start by tensing the muscles in your toes, hold it

for a few seconds, and then let go of the tension. Work your way up through your body, tensing and then relaxing each muscle group.

Journal Exercise:

Take a few moments to think about a recent time when you experienced a mood swing. Describe the situation in as much detail as possible. What triggered your mood to change?

How were you feeling before the mood swing?

1. How did your mood change (what did you start to feel)?

2. How did you handle your changing emotions?

3. What could you have done differently?

4. How do you think understanding mood swings can help you in the future?

☆ 4.2 HANDLING STRESS AND ANXIETY

In this chapter, we're going to chat about something that everyone experiences from time to time: stress and anxiety. Whether it's a big test at school, issues with friends, or just feeling overwhelmed by changes in your life, stress and anxiety can pop up. The great news is there are lots of ways to handle them. Let's explore how you can stay cool, calm, and collected.

Understanding Stress and Anxiety:

First off, what are stress and anxiety? Stress is your body's reaction to a challenge or demand. Anxiety is a feeling of fear or apprehension about what's to come. It's super normal to feel these emotions, especially as you grow and face new situations.

Identifying Your Stressors:

The first step in handling stress and anxiety is to figure out what's causing them. It could be school work, friendship troubles, changes at home, or even your own thoughts and worries. Once you identify these stressors, you can start finding ways to manage them.

Creating a Stress-Free Zone:

Find a place where you can relax and feel safe. It might be your room, a cozy corner of your house, or a spot in your garden. Fill it with things that make you happy, like your favorite books, a comfy pillow, or photos of fun memories.

Breathing and Relaxation Techniques:

Deep breathing can work wonders. Try this:

    ☆ Sit or lie down in a comfortable position.

    ☆ Slowly breathe in through your nose, counting to four.

    ☆ Hold your breath for a count of four.

    ☆ Slowly breathe out through your mouth for a count of four.

    ☆ Repeat several times.

You can also try relaxation apps that guide you through calming exercises or meditation.

Physical Activity:

Exercise isn't just good for your body; it's great for your mind, too. It releases chemicals called endorphins that make you feel good. Find activities that you enjoy, like dancing, biking, or even just a walk around the block.

Talk It Out:

Sometimes, the best way to handle stress is to talk about it. Find someone you trust, like a parent, teacher, or close friend, and share what you're feeling. Just voicing your worries can make them feel less overwhelming.

Keeping a Journal:

Writing down your thoughts and feelings can help you understand and manage them. You don't have to write every day, just whenever you feel like you need to unload your thoughts.

Time Management:

If schoolwork or activities are piling up, try making a schedule. Break down big tasks into smaller ones and set realistic goals. Remember, it's okay to say no if you're feeling overwhelmed.

Healthy Habits:

Eating well, getting enough sleep, and staying hydrated can all help manage stress and anxiety. Try to eat balanced meals, drink plenty of water, and get a good night's sleep.

Finding Your Happy Activities:

Do things that make you happy and help you relax. It could be drawing, listening to music, baking, or watching your favorite show. These activities are not just fun; they're a part of taking care of your mental health.

Learning Mindfulness:

Mindfulness is about living in the moment and being aware of your thoughts and feelings without judgment. You can practice this through simple activities like paying attention to your breath, eating slowly and savoring each bite, or noticing the sights and sounds during a walk.

Seeking Professional Help:

If your stress and anxiety feel too big to handle alone, it's okay to ask for help. A counselor, therapist, or doctor can provide support and guidance. There's absolutely no shame in seeking professional help; it's a brave and important step in taking care of your mental health.

TOPIC	SUMMARY
Understanding Stress and Anxiety	Stress is a reaction to a challenge, anxiety is apprehension about the future. Normal during growth and new situations.
Identifying Your Stressors	Figure out what's causing stress, like school or personal worries. Identifying helps in managing them.
Creating a Stress-Free Zone	Find a safe, relaxing space with comforting items. It can be a room or a spot outdoors.
Breathing and Relaxation Techniques	Practice deep breathing or use relaxation apps for calming. Helps in immediate stress relief.
Physical Activity	Exercise releases feel-good chemicals. Enjoyable activities like dancing or walking are beneficial.
Talk It Out	Discussing feelings with someone you trust can reduce overwhelm and provide relief.

TOPIC	SUMMARY
Keeping a Journal	Writing thoughts can clarify and help manage them. It's a tool for emotional unloading.
Time Management	Break tasks into smaller steps and set realistic goals. Learn to say no to avoid overload.
Healthy Habits	Balanced meals, sufficient sleep, and hydration are key to managing stress and anxiety.
Finding Your Happy Activities	Engage in activities you love for relaxation and mental health care.
Learning Mindfulness	Be present and aware of the current moment to reduce stress. Simple daily activities can aid in this.
Seeking Professional Help	If stress is too much, seek help from professionals. It's a strong and healthy decision.

Remember, handling stress and anxiety is a skill that takes practice. It's okay to have ups and downs. What's important is that you're taking steps to care for yourself. You're not alone in this journey, and there are many tools and people ready to support you. Keep being the wonderful, strong, and capable person you are, and know that you can handle whatever comes your way!

Journal Exercise:

I. Reflect on a recent situation where you felt stressed or anxious. Describe the situation in detail: who, what, when, where, and why.

2. Now, identify the physical signs you experienced during this situation. How did your body react? (eg. fast heartbeat, sweaty palms, etc.)

3. What were the thoughts running through your mind at that time? Write them down.

4. How did you handle this situation? Describe any strategies you used to manage your feelings. Did they work?

5. If you could go back to this situation, how would you handle your stress or anxiety differently, based on what you've learned in this chapter?

☆ 4.3 BUILDING A POSITIVE BODY IMAGE

Imagine you're looking into a mirror. You might notice your body is starting to look different. Maybe you're growing taller, or your hips are becoming wider. At times, you might feel like your body is no longer your own, but remember, it's all part of the journey to becoming the wonderful woman you're meant to be. Our society often sets expectations and standards of beauty that can be hard to live up to. You might see girls with perfect hair, flawless skin, and slender bodies in magazines or on social media, and you might start to think that you should look like them. But here's the secret: it's all airbrushed and edited. It's not real. What's real is you, in all of your uniqueness and individuality. So, you see, building a positive body image during puberty involves navigating these physical changes, grappling with your mental perception of yourself, and resisting the societal pressures to look a certain way. And believe it or not, it's possible to navigate this journey with confidence and positivity. After all, you're not just a girl; you're a butterfly in the making.

Remember this mantra: "I am beautiful, just as I am. I am strong. I am unique. I am me." Every time you feel uncertain or start comparing yourself to others, recite this mantra. It will remind you of your worth and beauty, just as you are.

Let's also look at some pointers to guide us:

- ☆ Try not to compare yourself to others. Each girl's puberty journey is unique, and there's no right or wrong way to go through it.

- ☆ Understand that what you see in the media isn't always real. Everyone is different, and that's what makes us beautiful.

- ☆ Embrace the changes that are happening to your body. They're a part of the amazing journey to becoming a woman.

- ☆ Remember it's completely normal to feel a range of emotions during puberty. It's okay to express these feelings and talk about them with someone you trust.

Let's take the story of a girl named Sarah. Sarah is an 11-year-old who loves to play basketball. She's the tallest girl in her class, and sometimes she feels different because of her height. One day, Sarah's mom noticed she was hunching over, trying to appear shorter. Sarah admitted that she wished she was shorter because some kids teased her about her height. Sarah's mom decided to address this situation constructively. Here's what they did:

1. Emphasizing Sarah's Strengths: Sarah's mom reminded her about the advantages of her height in basketball, how it made her a strong player. She spoke about famous basketball players who were tall and how their height was an asset, not a disadvantage. This helped Sarah to focus on the positive aspects of her height.

2. Affirmations: Every morning, Sarah and her mom did affirmations in front of the mirror. Sarah's mom would say, "I am strong, I am beautiful, I am tall and proud." Then,

Sarah would repeat the affirmations. This helped Sarah cultivate a positive perception of her body.

3. **The Uniqueness Project:** Sarah's mom encouraged her to start a project, interviewing different women who were tall and had succeeded in various fields. This project further instilled in Sarah the understanding that everyone is unique, and our unique features can be our strengths.

4. **Limiting Social Media:** Sarah's mom encouraged her to spend less time on social media and more time engaging in activities she loved. This helped Sarah to focus less on comparison and more on her passions and interests.

Now, let's bring this back to you. How can you apply these lessons to your life?

Emphasizing Your Strengths: Think about your unique features. Maybe you have freckles, curly hair, or a gap between your teeth. Instead of viewing these as flaws, recognize them as your signature features that make you, you! Write down three things that make you unique and special.

1. **Affirmations:** Stand in front of a mirror every morning and say out loud, "I am beautiful. I am unique. I love my body the way it is." It may feel strange at first, but these affirmations can help you cultivate a positive body image over time.

2. **The Uniqueness Project:** Start your own project celebrating the unique features of women you admire. You could draw pictures, write stories, or create a collage. This can help you understand that everyone is unique and beautiful in their own way.

3. **Limiting Social Media:** Try to spend less time browsing through pictures of 'perfect' bodies on social media. Instead, use that time to do something you love.

4. Remember, it's natural to have moments of self-doubt, but what's important is how you respond to those feelings. By embracing your unique features, practicing positive affirmations, celebrating uniqueness, and limiting comparison, you can cultivate a positive body image. It's all about loving and accepting yourself just as you are.

What's the one step you could take today to start building a more positive body image? Whatever it is, remember, you are beautiful just as you are.

Journal Exercise:

Reflect on a time when you felt really good about your physical self. Write a short paragraph about what you were doing, what you were wearing, and how you felt. Now list three actions you can take tomorrow to feel that positive feeling about your body again.

☆ 4.4 NURTURING HEALTHY FRIENDSHIPS

Have you heard the saying, "Show me your friends, and I'll tell you who you are"? This phrase highlights the weight of friendships in our lives, especially during adolescence, the magical time when you're no longer a child but not quite an adult either. Friendships aren't just about fun, sleepovers, or shared interests, they also shape who we are, how we see the world, and how we handle different situations. In this phase of your life, friendships become more rich and complex. They're like a small laboratory where you test your social skills, emotions, values, and how to handle disagreements. Every friendship is unique and has its own dynamics - the way you interact, communicate, and behave with each other. Understanding these dynamics is essential for fostering a healthy friendship. Take a moment to think about your interactions with your friends. What common patterns do you notice? Do you take turns deciding which games to play or movies to watch? Or does one friend often dominate the decision-making? Such patterns can help you better understand your friendships.

As your friendships deepen and become more complicated, you might also need to set boundaries. Boundaries are like invisible lines that help us understand where we end and where others begin. They help us express our needs and expectations in a friendship, and ensure we respect those of our friend. But setting boundaries doesn't mean pushing your friends away. It's more about preserving your wellbeing and the health of your friendship. In every friendship, conflicts are bound to happen. They aren't necessarily a bad thing. In fact, they can be an opportunity to learn more about your friends and yourself. The key is knowing how to deal with conflicts constructively. It's important to express how you feel and listen to your friend's viewpoint too. Always remember, it's not about who's right or wrong, but about finding a compromise that respects both of your feelings.

Keep in mind that friendships, like all relationships, change over time, and that's perfectly okay. As you grow and evolve, your interests, hobbies, or perspectives may shift, and that can impact your friendships. Some friendships may grow stronger, while others may fade. Remember, it's not about the quantity of friends you have, but the quality of the friendships.

Let's imagine a scenario. You and your best friend, Mia, have been inseparable since kindergarten. But since the school year started, you've noticed she's been hanging out with the 'cool' girls and hasn't been spending as much time as before with you. You feel left out and a little hurt.

Identify Your Feelings: The first step in dealing with this situation is recognizing your emotions. You might feel a mix of sadness, confusion, and even a tad bit of jealousy. That's normal and alright. It's okay to feel confused and upset. It's important to not bottle these feelings up.

1. Express Your Feelings: Once you're sure about your feelings, it's time to express them. It's a delicate conversation, so choose your words wisely. You could tell Mia something like, "I've noticed we haven't been hanging out as much. I miss spending time with you. Is everything alright?" By doing this, you're not accusing her of anything, but simply expressing how you feel.

2. Listen: After expressing your feelings, give Mia a chance to explain her side of the story. She might have a reason you're not aware of. It's key to be open-minded and understanding.

3. Now, let's consider another scenario. Imagine your friend, Alex, is going through a tough time at home. She doesn't feel comfortable talking about it, and her behavior has been erratic lately.

Show Empathy: In such a situation, it's important to show empathy. Empathy is the ability to understand and share someone else's feelings. Even if you don't know exactly what Alex is going through, you could say, „I can tell you're not feeling your best, just know that I'm here for you."

1. Offer Support: Extend your help to Alex. Offering to spend more time with her or simply listening to her can be a great comfort. Remember, it's not about fixing her problems, but about supporting her through them.

2. Respect Her Space: If Alex is not ready to open up about her problems, respect her space. It's important to give her room to process her feelings on her own terms.

Lastly, let's think about a situation where you and your friend, Sam, have had a disagreement. You both have different opinions about an issue and can't seem to agree.

1. **Keep Calm:** First, try to keep calm and avoid escalating the situation. Losing your temper won't help resolve anything.

2. **Communicate:** State your point of view without trying to attack Sam's opinions. Use phrases like, "From my perspective..." or "I feel that...". This shows respect for Sam's point of view.

3. **Agree to Disagree:** Sometimes, it's okay to agree to disagree. Friends don't always have to agree on everything. What matters is respecting each other's viewpoints.

These situations, strategies, and exercises are designed to guide you on your friendship journey. Maintaining a healthy friendship involves empathy, respect, honesty, and understanding. In the end, every friendship is unique, and it's this uniqueness that makes our friendships so special.

Journal Exercise:

1. Write down the names of your three closest friends. For each friend, list three qualities that you admire about them and why these qualities are important to you.

2. Reflect on a recent situation where you had a disagreement or misunderstanding with a friend. How did you handle it and what could have been done differently?

3. Think of a time when a friend was there for you when you needed them most. Write about that experience and the emotions you felt.

4. Identify one way you feel that your friendships have evolved as part of growing up. What changes have you noticed? How do these changes make you feel?

5. Consider your future self. What kind of friend do you want to be as you navigate through puberty? Write a letter to your future self about the kind of friendship values you want to uphold.

☆ 4.5 THE IMPACT OF SOCIAL MEDIA ON EMOTIONS

As you start growing up, you'll notice a growing interest in connecting with your friends and other people from all over the world. Social media can be lots of fun, allowing you to share your interests, experiences, and thoughts, or to keep up with the latest trends. But remember, everything in life has a flip side. And for social media, it's the way it can influence your emotions during your journey through puberty. Puberty is a time of great change, not just for your body, but for your emotions as well. As you navigate this stage, you might find yourself more sensitive to the world around you, and this includes the digital world of social media. The way you interact with social media and the content you encounter can have a significant effect on how you feel.

Just imagine scrolling down your feed and seeing a picture of your friend having the time of their life at a party you weren't invited to. Or, perhaps, seeing posts of picture-perfect models and celebrities, and then glancing at your reflection in the mirror. These digital experiences can lead to a whirlwind of emotions, ranging from sadness and jealousy to self-doubt and anxiety. But why does social media have this power over our emotions? There are a few reasons.

Social media is a highlight reel of people's lives. Most people only share their best moments, like their vacations, achievements, and happy gatherings. This can create an illusion that everyone else's life is perfect, leading you to compare your own life with theirs, which can cause feelings of inadequacy or dissatisfaction.

1. Social media can often feel like a popularity contest. The number of likes, comments, and followers you have can seem like a measure of your worth. This can breed a lot of stress and anxiety, especially if you feel like you're not getting enough attention or approval from your peers.

2. The anonymity and distance that social media provides can sometimes embolden people to behave unkindly or insensitively. Cyberbullying and negative comments can lead to feelings of hurt, sadness, and anger.

Imagine this: Emily, a 10-year-old girl, sees posts of her favorite celebrity always dressed in fancy clothes, having glamorous parties, and living a seemingly perfect life. This makes her feel unhappy with her own life and causes her to compare herself to others.

1. Recognizing Unhealthy Comparison: Emily needs to know that it's normal to compare ourselves to others, but it can be harmful if it makes us unhappy with what we have.

2. Reality Check: She should remind herself that what she sees on social media is often a highlight reel. Most people only post their best moments, not their daily struggles or ordinary moments.

3. Focusing on the Positive: Emily could start a gratitude journal where she writes down things she's thankful for. This can shift her focus from what she lacks to what she has.

4. Limiting Social Media Use: She might set boundaries for her social media use. This could include specified times

for using social media and ensuring she spends more time doing activities she loves.

In this situation, it is essential to understand that people present idealized versions of their lives on social media, which may not reflect their real-world experiences. It's important to engage in healthy online behavior by setting boundaries, not comparing our lives with others, and communicating our feelings when necessary. By doing so, social media can become a tool for connection, rather than a source of emotional turmoil. And it's okay to unfollow accounts that make you feel bad about yourself and to take breaks when necessary. Your emotional health is important, both online and offline.

Journal Exercise:

1. Write about a time when something you saw on social media made you feel good and a time when it made you feel bad. Why do you think you felt that way?

2. Consider the amount of time you spend on social media. How might your day change if you reduced that time by half? What activities could you do instead?

3. List three positive and three negative effects of social media on your life. How can you maximize the positive and manage the negative effects?

Chapter 5
SOCIAL DYNAMICS AND RELATIONSHIPS

☆ 5.1 FAMILY DYNAMICS DURING PUBERTY

Puberty is a transformative time, not just for you but also for your entire family. As you grow and change, the dynamics of your family may start to shift. This period of growth is like a dance, where everyone is learning new steps and trying to find their rhythm.

When it comes to your emotional changes, you might notice that your feelings seem more intense or unpredictable. This can be a bit confusing for your family as well. They might be used to you being cheerful and energetic, and now find you need more quiet time or sometimes seem moody. It's important to remember that they are learning and adjusting too. Your social changes, on the other hand, involve how you interact with the people around you. You may start to crave more independence, wanting to make more of your own decisions. It's a part of growing up, and while it can be exciting, it can also feel a bit intimidating. Your desire for independence could lead to some changes at home. For example, the time you used to spend playing board games with your family might now be spent talking on the phone with friends. Or instead of always going along on family outings, you may want to spend time doing things on your own or with your friends. These shifts can lead to new dynamics within your family.

Imagine this: You are sitting with your family at the dinner table, and you notice that your little brother is poking fun at your recent mood swings. You've been feeling a little more emotional lately, which is completely normal and part of puberty. However, dealing with your brother's teasing can feel frustrating, and it's crucial to handle such instances carefully. Here's what you can do:

1. Express your feelings: Politely explain to your brother that his comments are hurting your feelings. Usually, family members don't mean to upset us, and when they realize they've done so, they apologize and rectify their behavior.

2. Reach out to your parents: Your parents are there to support and guide you through these life changes. Let them know how your brother's teasing is making you feel. They can help create a better understanding with your sibling about your emotional changes during puberty.

Now, let's take a look at a different scenario. Maybe you've noticed some physical changes, like developing breasts, and you're feeling a bit shy about it. You're not alone; many girls feel this way. Here are some steps you can take to navigate this situation:

1. Decide who to talk to: You may feel more comfortable discussing this with a person who's been through the same changes, like your mom, an aunt, or an older sister.

2. Express your concerns: It's perfectly okay to feel uncertain or worried about these changes. Let them know how you're feeling, and ask any questions you have.

Remember, your family is there to support you during this significant stage of your life. While it might feel awkward at first to talk about these changes, having open discussions can help everyone understand what you're going through and offer more empathetic support.

Here's a simple exercise you can do to foster a more open communication environment at home:

★ „Family Discussion Night": Set aside a time every week when your family sits down to talk about any issues, changes, or exciting things happening in their lives. This could be a safe space where you can express your feelings about the changes you're experiencing. To make sure everyone gets a chance to speak, you could:

1. Use a talking stick: The person holding the stick gets the floor to talk without interruptions. This encourages active listening and respect towards each speaker's thoughts and feelings.

2. Implement a 'no judgment' rule: Everyone should feel comfortable sharing without fear of being judged or criticized.

Communication is key during this time of significant change. It's okay to feel confused or overwhelmed. Reach out to your family, share your feelings, and ask questions. You're not alone; your family is there to support you during your journey through puberty.

Journal Exercise:

1. Write about a recent situation at home where you noticed a change in the dynamics of your relationship with your family. How did that make you feel?

2. Reflect on a conversation you had with your parents about puberty that was hard for you. What made it challenging? How would you approach it differently?

3. List three questions you wish you could ask your family about puberty, but are too embarrassed or afraid to ask. Are there alternative ways or people you could get this information from?

☆ 5.2 FRIENDSHIPS: OLD AND NEW

As we grow and change, so do our friendships. Just like our bodies and minds, our relationships with others also experience transformations. It's quite normal and to be expected. After all, everyone is growing up at the same time, navigating through the same stage of life - puberty. During puberty friendships often deepen. This can mean that your circle of friends may change or evolve. You may find yourself wanting to spend more time with certain friends who understand you better. Or perhaps, you're drawn towards new friends who have similar interests or who are going through the same changes. It's all part of discovering who you are and where you fit in. As you become more emotionally mature, you might find yourself becoming more empathetic. This can also affect your friendships, as it allows you to connect with your friends on a deeper level, strengthening the bond you share. Also, during puberty, you may start to value privacy more. This can play a role in your friendships as well. You might start sharing secrets and personal feelings with your friends, developing a sense of trust and confidentiality. This can give your friendships a new level of depth and meaning.

Navigating friendships during puberty can feel like steering a ship through a storm at times, but you are the captain of your friendship ship, and you're equipped to handle any stormy weather. Let's look at some situations that could come up, and how you might manage them using practical exercises and strategies.

Consider Lucy and Jane, who've been best friends since kindergarten. They've always been in the same classes, had the same hobbies, and even liked the same foods. But now that they're both entering puberty, things are starting to change. Lucy's become more interested in sports, while Jane has developed a passion for art and painting. They're starting to drift apart, and both are feeling lost and confused.

If you find yourself in a similar situation, remember that it's perfectly normal for interests to change and diverge as you grow up. It can be a bit scary, but it's also a chance to learn more about yourself and explore new things.

1. Open Communication: Have an honest conversation with your friend. Tell her about your feelings, and listen to hers. It's common to feel scared or anxious about losing a friend, but often, just talking about it can help.

2. Find Common Ground: Even though Lucy enjoys sports and Jane loves art, they can still find activities they both like. They might discover a shared love for animals, or a TV show, or a type of food. Look for common ground and make an effort to spend time doing those things together.

Now, let's think about Mia and Ava. They're also best friends. Mia is developing faster physically than Ava, which is making Ava feel uncomfortable and left behind. If you're feeling like Ava, or if you're in Mia's shoes, here are some things you can do:

1. Be Understanding: Remember that everyone develops at their own pace during puberty. If you're developing faster, try to be patient and understanding with your friend who may be feeling self-conscious or left behind. If you're developing slower, know that there's nothing wrong with you - your time will come, too.

2. Stay Supportive: Try to reassure your friend that you're still the same person, even if your bodies are changing. Remind them that true friendship isn't based on looks but on shared experiences, trust, and kindness.

Lastly, consider a situation where a new friend comes into your life. Let's say Lisa, who's new to your school, starts spending a lot of time with your best friend Sarah. You might feel jealous or left out. But it's important to remember that it's completely okay for your friend to make new friends. Here's what you can do:

1. Be Open-Minded: Instead of seeing Lisa as a threat, try to get to know her more. She could become a new friend to you as well.

2. Talk About It: If your feelings of being left out persist, talk to Sarah about it. She might not even be aware that you're feeling this way, and a heart-to-heart chat could help clear things up.

Remember, friendships during puberty can be a rollercoaster, but with open communication, patience, and understanding, you can ride the ups and downs and come out stronger on the other side.

Journal Exercise:

1. List down five attributes that you believe make a good friend. Explain why you think each attribute is important.

2. Think about your old friends. How have those friendships changed as you grow? Write about a memorable moment you experienced with an old friend.

3. Now, think about some of the new friendships you're developing. Write about why these friendships are important to you.

4. Can you identify any differences between your old and new friendships? Write about these differences and why you think they exist.

☆ 5.3 DEALING WITH BULLYING AND PEER PRESSURE

Every girl's journey to adulthood is marked with many changes and challenges. Among these hurdles, bullying and peer pressure are two significant issues. But what exactly are they? And how are they different? Bullying is an act where someone intentionally causes harm to another person, either physically, verbally, or emotionally. It may be a single incident or a recurring pattern of behavior. This might mean calling someone mean names, spreading rumors, excluding them from activities, or even physically hurting them. Peer pressure, on the other hand, is a feeling which pushes you to do something or behave in a certain way because you think it's what your friends expect from you. It could be feeling coerced to wear a particular type of clothing or join certain activities, even if you're not comfortable with it. These two can sometimes overlap; for example, a group of friends could gang up and push you to do something you don't want to do. If you refuse, they might resort to bullying, like name-calling or spreading rumors about you. The effects of bullying and peer pressure can be far-reaching. Here's how they might influence your mental and emotional health during puberty:

1. Self-esteem: Bullies often target personal characteristics, which can make you feel self-conscious and lead to a drop in self-esteem. Peer pressure, too, can make you feel inadequate if you can't meet the expectations set by your friends.

2. Fear and Anxiety: Bullying can make you fearful of going to school or certain social situations. Peer pressure can induce anxiety as you struggle to fit in and conform to group norms.

3. Loneliness and Isolation: If you're being bullied, or if you resist peer pressure, you may find yourself ostracized, leading to feelings of loneliness.

4. Depression: Continuous bullying and the strain of constant peer pressure can contribute to feelings of hopelessness, sadness, and even depression.

5. Academic Performance: The stress from bullying and peer pressure can negatively affect concentration and interest in school, leading to a drop in grades and academic performance.

Let's imagine a scenario where you're at school during lunch break. You're sitting with your friends when a girl from another class comes over. She starts making fun of your clothes, saying they're not cool, and everyone starts laughing. This is a form of bullying, and it can feel really terrible.

Now, let's take a look at how you might handle this situation:

1. Stay Calm: The first instinct is to get defensive, but take a deep breath and compose yourself. Remember, getting

upset is what the bully wants. If you stay calm, you're already taking away their power.

2. **Stand Up for Yourself:** Once you're calm, you can look at her and say, "I like my clothes. It's okay if you don't. We all have different tastes." You're standing up for yourself without being mean or aggressive.

3. **Seek Help:** After this incident, it's important to tell a trusted adult, like your teacher or parent, about what happened. They can provide guidance and ensure the bullying stops.

Let's look at another scenario. You're at a sleepover and everyone decides they want to watch a scary movie. You don't like scary movies, but you don't want to be the only one who doesn't watch. This is peer pressure. Even though it's not as serious as bullying, it can still be uncomfortable.

Here's how you can manage this situation:

1. **Be Honest:** Tell your friends you don't enjoy scary movies. It's okay to have different likes and dislikes.

2. **Suggest Alternatives:** Maybe you could all watch a comedy or an adventure movie instead. Offering a solution shows you're not just being difficult.

3. **Stick to Your Decision:** If your friends still insist on the scary movie, you don't have to give in. You could read a book or play a game on your phone while they watch the movie.

To better equip yourself to deal with bullying and peer pressure, try practicing these strategies at home.

★ **Role Play:** Ask a family member or a trusted friend to role-play different scenarios with you. This can help you become more comfortable standing up for yourself and expressing your thoughts.

★ Journaling: Write down your feelings after each practice session in a journal. Over time, this will help you understand your emotions better and give you insight into why you react a certain way in different situations.

★ Calming Techniques: Practice deep breathing and other calming techniques regularly. This can help you manage your emotions in tense situations and allow you to respond calmly and confidently.

There is no one-size-fits-all solution to dealing with bullying or peer pressure. Every situation is unique. But by practicing these strategies and exercises, you'll be well-prepared to handle these challenges. Although it may seem tough at first, with time and practice, you'll find it easier to stand up for yourself and resist peer pressure.

Journal Exercise:

Reflect on a time when you experienced or witnessed bullying or peer pressure. Write down where you were, who was involved, and what happened. Then, think about how you handled that situation. If a similar situation were to happen in the future, what would you do differently?

Additionally, list five ways you can resist peer pressure, and how you might help a friend who is being bullied. Write a pledge to yourself to help create a safe environment where respect is the norm and bullying is out of bounds. How can you stand up for yourself and others?

☆ 5.4 UNDERSTANDING CRUSHES AND ROMANTIC FEELINGS

As you grow up, your body isn't the only thing that changes. Your feelings change too. You might start to notice that you're feeling different about certain people. You know, like when your heart seems to pound a little louder when they're near, or how you can't help but smile every time they speak. These feelings are often referred to as having a "crush" or experiencing "romantic feelings." As you move into your puberty years, your emotions begin to mature just as your body does. You start to develop deeper feelings for people, and sometimes, these feelings can be romantic.

So, where do these crushes and romantic feelings come from? Well, as you reach puberty, your brain starts releasing a whole bunch of different hormones. These hormones are like little messengers that tell your body to grow and change. But they also influence your emotions, which is why you might start developing these new, intense feelings. Essentially, having a crush or romantic feelings for someone means that you have a strong emotional attraction towards them. You might find them physically attractive, or you might be drawn to their personality, or both! Whether it's their sparkling eyes, infectious laugh, or the way they're always kind to everyone, there's something about them that just makes your heart flutter.

But it's not all butterflies and daydreams. Sometimes, crushes can feel overwhelming, especially if you're not sure if the other person feels the same way about you. You might feel nervous around them, constantly worry about what they think of you, or even become a bit obsessed. It's important to remember that it's okay to have these feelings, but it's equally important not to let them consume you. And what about relationships during this time? Well, having a crush can definitely impact your relationships. You might spend more time thinking about or trying to spend time with the person you have a crush on, which could affect your relationships with your other friends. Plus, as you start to explore these romantic feelings, you might start having disagreements or misunderstandings with your friends, especially if you all have a crush on the same person.

But, while crushes can sometimes lead to drama, they also help you grow. They teach you how to deal with complex emotions, how to handle disappointment if your feelings aren't returned, and how to navigate the exciting, new world of romantic relationships. In short, crushes and romantic feelings, though confusing at times, are an essential part of your journey towards becoming a teenager.

Let's imagine... You're in math class, minding your own business, when suddenly your heart starts to race. The cause? The new kid in class, Alex, just walked in. Every time you see Alex, your stomach does somersaults and your palms get sweaty. This, my friend, is what people often call a 'crush'.

Here's a step-by-step guide on how you can navigate these new feelings:

1. Acknowledge Your Feelings: It's okay to have a crush. It's a totally normal part of growing up. Admitting to yourself that you have a crush can help you make sense of what you're feeling.

2. Understand Your Feelings: Analyze what it is about this person that's causing these fluttery feelings. Is it because they're kind, smart, funny, or just really good at soccer? Identifying these qualities can help you understand what you value in people, which can be helpful in the future.

3. Keep Things in Perspective: Remember, having a crush is not the same as being in love. It's fun to daydream, but keep in mind that people are not perfect. Alex might look

like a movie star and solve algebra problems like a genius, but they might also have habits that annoy you.

4. **Practice Self-Control:** It's easy to get carried away with your feelings and make your crush the center of your universe. Don't let this happen. Keep living your life, spend time with friends, continue with your hobbies, and focus on your schoolwork.

5. **Share Your Feelings:** If you're comfortable, talk to someone you trust about your feelings. It could be a best friend, a sibling, or even a parent or a guardian. They can provide a comforting ear, a bit of advice, or a much-needed reality check.

Now, let's explore a situation where you're really struggling with your crush feelings. Maybe Alex has started dating someone else, or perhaps they've moved to another town. You feel like your heart's been torn apart. Here are some tips on how to handle these tough situations:

★ Feel Your Feelings: It's okay to feel upset, disappointed, or even heartbroken. These feelings are normal and won't last forever, even if it feels like they will right now.

★ Distract Yourself: Engage in activities you enjoy, like reading a good book, playing soccer, or painting. Keeping yourself occupied can help distract you from your feelings of sadness.

★ Reach Out to Others: Talk to your friends and family. They can provide comfort, perspective, and even a few laughs.

★ Stay Active: Physical activity helps our bodies release chemicals that can make us feel happier and more relaxed. Try dancing, skating, biking, or even just going for a walk.

★ Practice Self-Care: Make sure you're eating well, getting enough sleep, and taking care of your hygiene. It's easy to neglect these things when you're feeling down, but they're important for your overall well-being.

Lastly, let's say you're ready to confess your feelings to Alex. You're terrified, but you feel like you can't keep it a secret any longer. Here's what you can do:

1. **Plan What to Say:** Think about what you want to say beforehand. Keep it simple and honest.

2. **Choose the Right Time and Place:** Find a quiet, private place and make sure Alex is not in a rush or stressed out.

3. **Be Brave:** It's normal to be nervous, but remember that it takes a lot of courage to express your feelings.

4. **Be Prepared for Any Response:** Alex might feel the same, they might not, or they might need time to think. All these responses are okay.

5. **Respect Their Feelings:** If Alex doesn't feel the same way, that's okay. It might hurt, but everyone has the right to their own feelings.

STEP	ACTION	PURPOSE
Acknowledge Your Feelings	Admit to yourself that you have a crush.	Helps in recognizing and accepting your emotions.
Understand Your Feelings	Analyze the qualities in the person that attract you.	Aids in understanding what you value in others.
Keep Things in Perspective	Remember crushes are not the same as being in love.	Keeps your expectations realistic and grounded.

STEP	ACTION	PURPOSE
Practice Self-Control	Focus on your life, hobbies, friends, and schoolwork.	Ensures your crush doesn't overshadow other important aspects of your life.
Share Your Feelings	Talk to a trusted person about your feelings.	Provides comfort, advice, or a new perspective.
Handling Tough Situations	Stay active, engage in enjoyable activities, and talk to friends and family.	Helps in coping with disappointment or heartache.
Confessing Your Feelings	Plan your words, choose a calm setting, and be brave but prepared for any response.	Allows you to express your feelings honestly and openly.
Journal Exercise	List emotions related to your crush and write a hypothetical story about an interaction.	Facilitates deeper emotional exploration and self-awareness.

Everyone experiences crushes and romantic feelings differently. There's no right or wrong way to have a crush. The most important thing is that you handle these feelings in fantastic ways and take care of your emotional health.

Journal Exercise:

List three emotions that you feel when you have a crush. For each emotion, write a sentence on why you think you might be feeling that way. Remember, it's perfectly natural and healthy to feel different emotions about different people. You're just starting to understand and explore these feelings!

Followed by this, write a story about your crush in a very hypothetical situation where you'd be interacting with them. How would you want them to respond to you? Why?

☆ 5.5 BALANCING ONLINE AND IN-PERSON RELATIONSHIPS

Making connections with others is one of the most wonderful and exciting parts of growing up. As you grow older, you'll find that there are many ways to build friendships, both online and in person. Both types of relationships can be rewarding and fulfilling, but they also need to be balanced in a way that suits you best. One significant difference between online and in-person friendships is how we spend our time. For instance, when you're hanging out with your friends after school, you're spending time in person. On the other hand, when you chat with your friends on the internet or play games together online, you're spending time in an online setting. Each has its perks: in-person interactions allow for deeper bonding through shared experiences, while online connections allow us to stay in touch no matter where we are.

It's essential to manage your time wisely. Too much online interaction can take away from the valuable experiences of in-person friendships, like the spontaneous joy of a shared laugh or the comfort of a shoulder to lean on. Likewise, too much in-person interaction can make you feel detached from the online world, where many of your peers might be connecting and sharing experiences. Another important factor in balancing online and in-person relationships is privacy. When you're connecting with friends online, it's easy to share photos, messages, and thoughts with just a click. But remember, once something is out on the internet, it's not within your control anymore. This doesn't mean you must be secretive or shy away from sharing online. Instead, it's about being mindful of what you share and with whom you share it. On the contrary, in-person friendships can offer a sense of privacy that is more controlled and immediate. Also, consider your emotional wellness. Online, we can control how we present ourselves, which can be both empowering and stressful. It can be easy to compare ourselves to others based on what we see online, but remember, people often share the best parts of their lives, not the everyday moments or hardships. In-person relationships, however, provide direct emotional feedback and support, which is crucial for our emotional growth and well-being.

To help you understand how to balance online and in-person relationships, let's walk through the story of Lily, a ten-year-old girl who loves playing online games and hanging out with her friends after school. Lily loved spending time online playing her favorite game, "Fantastic Fairy World", and chatting with her friends. However, she also enjoyed hanging out with her friends in the park after school, laughing, and sharing stories. As she got busier with schoolwork and extracurricular activities, she found it challenging to find equilibrium between her online and in-person friendships. To manage her time more effectively, Lily:

★ Set a daily limit for her online game. She decided to spend no more than one hour each day on „Fantastic Fairy World".

★ Made sure to spend quality time with her in-person friends after school, setting aside specific days for park visits.

Concerned about privacy, Lily:

★ Decided not to share any personal details, such as her school name or exact location, within the game or online chats.

★ Only shared photos and messages online with her trusted friends, those she knew well and had met in person.

To ensure her emotional wellness, Lily:

☆ Reminded herself that people only share the best parts of their lives online. She knew that it was normal not to have exciting news or beautiful photos to post every day.

☆ Made an effort to express her feelings honestly with her in-person friends, appreciating the immediate emotional feedback and support she received.

Through these actions, Lily found a balance that worked for her, allowing her to enjoy both her online and in-person friendships. She learned that it's not the quantity of time spent, but the quality of connections that matter the most.

Let's look at one more example: Imagine you're having a typical day at school, filled with classes, lunchtime, and friends. After school, you come home, finish your homework, and have some free time. How do you choose to spend it? If you're like many girls your age, you might turn to your computer or smartphone, eager to check your social media or join your online gaming community. Let's take a closer look at this scenario and see how you can balance your online and in-person relationships. You've just come home from school and you're ready to relax. It's been a long day and the thought of visiting your favorite virtual world or chatting with your online friends seems appealing. At the same time, your little sister wants to play a board game.

Balancing these two interactions could look like this:

☆ Set a timer and dedicate some time to both activities. You might play with your sister for 30 minutes, then spend another 30 minutes online. This way, you're nurturing both your real-life and online relationships.

☆ Consider including your sister in your online activities. Maybe she'd enjoy being part of your virtual world, or she might find the game you're playing interesting. This way, you're spending quality time together and enjoying your online interests.

Now, imagine another scenario. It's the weekend, and you're part of an online study group for an upcoming science project. You also have a family dinner later in the day. How can you manage both? Here's a possible approach:

1. Plan your online study group early in the day. This gives you plenty of time to contribute and helps ensure that your online commitments won't clash with your in-person ones.

2. Let your family know about your study group. They might be able to help create a quiet space for you to focus, and they'll be aware of your commitments too.

Another day, you're ready to spend hours painting, an activity you enjoy, but you also want to check your social media feeds and engage with your online friends. What should you do?

Here's how you might handle this situation:

★ Set specific times for your painting and your online activities. You could paint in the morning when you're feeling fresh and creative, then check your social media in the afternoon.

★ Share your painting progress on your social media. This way, you're combining your online and in-person interests, and you might even inspire your friends to take up painting too!

These are just examples. Your life will have its own unique situations and challenges, and it's important to find a balance that works for you. Remember, it's not about choosing between online and in-person relationships, but about finding ways to enjoy and nurture both. Just as you need to eat a balanced diet for your body's health, you need a balanced 'social diet' for your emotional health. That includes a mix of online and in-person interactions, time spent alone, and time spent in groups, time for learning, and time for fun. So, next time you're faced with a choice between online and in-person activities, remember these examples, and think about how you can create your own balanced social diet. It's a skill that will help you now, and for many years to come.

Journal Exercise:

1. After reading this chapter, list down five ways that online and in-person relationships are similar and five ways they are different.

2. Think about one of your online and one of your in-person friendships. How do you manage these friendships differently? Are there differences in the type of respect and attention you give to each? Why do you think that is?

3. Imagine a situation where a friend online treated you badly, and another where a friend in-person did the same. How would your reaction be similar or different in both situations?

4. Reflect on a situation where an in-person friendship had a conflict and compare it with an online friendship conflict. How were they resolved differently?

Chapter 6
CULTIVATING HEALTHY HABITS

☆ 6.1 THE ROLE OF NUTRITION AND EXERCISE

What you choose to eat and how often you move your body can have a big impact, especially in the changing times of puberty. These are like the secret ingredients to your growth recipe. They help build the best version of you, not only physically, but also mentally and emotionally. Just like a car needs the right type of fuel to run smoothly, your body also needs the right kind of nutrients to function at its best. When we talk about nutrition, we're referring to the vitamins, minerals, proteins, carbohydrates, and fats that you get from the foods you eat. Each of these plays a unique part in helping your body grow and develop.

Vitamins and minerals support your overall health and can help your body get energy from food. They play a vital role in ensuring your bones grow strong and your brain functions properly.

★ Proteins are the building blocks of your body. They help to build, maintain, and repair tissues in your body - including those vital muscles!

★ Carbohydrates provide your body with energy. They're like the gas that keeps your body's engine running throughout the day.

★ Fats are also an important energy source and they're essential for brain development. They help your body absorb vitamins and protect your organs.

Now, let's not forget about exercise! Exercise is just as important as nutrition. It's like the key that starts the car's engine. Regular physical activity helps to strengthen your bones and muscles, maintain a healthy weight, and even boost your mood. The type of exercise you do can also have different effects on your body. For example, weight-bearing exercises like running, dancing, or playing soccer are good for bone health. They can help to make your bones stronger and reduce the risk of fractures. On the other hand, exercises like swimming, cycling, or yoga are great for flexibility and cardiovascular health. It's important to note that nutrition and exercise can also play a big role in how you feel about your body. When you eat a balanced diet and are active regularly, you're more likely to feel good about yourself and your changing body. So, remember, the changes that are happening to your body during puberty are completely natural. Being mindful of your nutrition and finding ways to stay active can help support these changes and make you feel good inside and out!

Let's take a closer look at how nutrition and exercise can be practically applied to your daily life. To truly understand how this works, let's imagine a girl named Lily. Lily is ten years old, and she's starting to notice changes in her body. She's becoming more conscious about her health and wellbeing, especially as she starts to grow up. So with Lily as our guide, let's explore some concrete examples, real-life scenarios and exercises she can implement. For starters, Lily knows she needs to eat a balanced diet. She understands that her body needs a variety of nutrients to grow and develop. Here's what her meals might look like:

☆ For breakfast, she might have a bowl of whole-grain cereal with a banana and a glass of low-fat milk. This meal provides her with fiber, potassium and calcium, all essential nutrients for her growing body.

☆ Lunch could be a turkey sandwich on whole grain bread, with lettuce, tomatoes and a side of carrots. This gives Lily protein, more fiber, and plenty of vitamins.

☆ For dinner, Lily's mom might make grilled chicken with a side of broccoli and brown rice. These foods provide protein, Vitamin C, and more fiber.

★ Lily also knows the importance of hydration, so she drinks plenty of water throughout the day and avoids sugary drinks.

Now, let's talk about exercise. Lily loves to play soccer with her friends after school. This kind of activity is great because it helps Lily develop her strength, coordination, and overall fitness level. Plus, it's a lot of fun! Lily also likes to do a few simple exercises at home, like:

1. Jumping jacks: They increase her heart rate and improve her cardiovascular fitness.

2. Squats: They help build her leg and core strength, which is important for everyday activities and sports.

3. Push-ups: They help build upper body and core strength.

Let's imagine a typical day for Lily. After a nutritious breakfast, she bikes to school, giving her a good amount of physical activity first thing in the morning. At lunch, she chooses a healthy option from the cafeteria, remembering what she learned about balanced meals. After school, she has soccer practice, where she runs around and stays active. When she gets home, she does her homework, eats a balanced dinner, and does a bit of exercising – perhaps ten jumping jacks, ten squats, and ten push-ups. In this way, Lily is maintaining a balanced diet and regular exercise routine. But remember, everybody is different, and what works for Lily might not work for everyone else. The key is to find healthy foods you enjoy and activities you love. By doing so, you'll be taking great care of your body and mind as they change and grow during puberty. Remember, being healthy is not about being perfect. It's about making good choices most of the time, staying active and having fun.

Journal Exercise:

I. List three important things you learned about nutrition and exercise in this chapter.

I. What are three ways you think you could improve your own diet or exercise routines?

2. Can you identify one unhealthy eating or exercise habit you currently have? Write down some steps you can take to change this.

☆ 6.2 THE IMPORTANCE OF SLEEP

Imagine a magical time machine. It takes you on a journey every night, helping you grow taller, think smarter, and feel happier when you wake up. This isn't something from a sci-fi movie; it's something you use every night. It's sleep! During puberty, your body and mind are undergoing a lot of changes, and sleep is the magic fuel that powers this transformation. Like a nightly reboot for your brain and body, sleep is more than just resting after a day of school, sports, or play. It's a critical period when your body gets busy with some important work. Sleep plays a key role in your physical growth. As you snooze, your body releases a hormone called human growth hormone (HGH). This hormone is like a master key that unlocks your growth potential, helping you to grow taller and stronger. It also aids in muscle development and repair, perfect for those days when you've done a bit of extra physical activity.

But that's not all. Sleep is also a superstar when it comes to your brain. As you drift off into dreamland, your brain doesn't switch off. Instead, it starts sorting and storing all the information you've gathered during the day. This process helps improve your memory, concentration, and decision-making skills. And remember those tricky math problems or complex sentences that seemed impossible to understand? With a good night's sleep, your brain can solve those puzzles while you dream, making learning easier the next day. Sleep is like a comforting friend, helping you navigate the ups and downs of your emotions. Puberty can sometimes feel like a roller coaster ride, with happiness, excitement, confusion, and mood swings all in one go. A good night's sleep can help keep this ride smooth by regulating the chemicals and hormones that influence your emotions and mood.

Sounds like a magic potion, doesn't it? Well, that's because sleep is indeed magical! Now that you understand how important sleep is for your growing body, mind, and emotions, the next step is to learn how to ensure you're getting enough quality sleep.

Let's imagine a routine day in the life of our friend Lily. Lily has a typical day with school, homework, and extracurricular activities to keep her busy. Let's look at how sleep, or lack of it, affects her day.

★ Lily starts her day with a groan when her alarm clock blares at 7 am. She only managed to fall asleep around midnight after a long internet surfing session. She manages to drag herself to school but, by mid-morning, she feels exhausted and cranky. She finds it hard to concentrate during lessons, and by lunchtime, she can barely keep her eyes open.

★ She stumbles through the rest of the school day in a daze, struggling to remember her class lessons and making several careless mistakes in her work. By late afternoon, she's too tired to enjoy her favorite dance class and makes more mistakes than usual.

★ When she gets home, Lily has to do her homework. But she's so tired that a task that would normally take her half an hour takes twice as long. Lily goes to bed late again, and the cycle continues.

Now, let's see how a good night's sleep changes Lily's day.

* ★ With a peaceful night's sleep under her belt, Lily wakes up to her alarm feeling refreshed and alert. She heads off to school, excited about the day ahead. She pays attention in class, absorbs new information easily, and even has the energy to participate in discussions.

* ★ Her improved focus and sharp memory help her excel in her schoolwork. She doesn't make those careless mistakes, and her academic performance improves.

* ★ She also enjoys her dance class more because she's not exhausted. Her coordination is better, and she remembers all the dance steps.

* ★ At home, she finishes her homework efficiently, giving her time to relax and unwind before bed. She goes to bed at a decent hour, ensuring she gets enough sleep for the next day.

Do you see the difference sleep can make in Lily's life? The same happens in your life too! So, what can Lily, and you, do to ensure a good night's sleep?

1. Create a Bedtime Routine: A regular routine going to bed at the same time every night, even on weekends, helps train your body to follow a consistent sleep pattern.

2. Limit Screen Time Before Bed: The light from screens can interfere with the production of melatonin, a hormone that regulates sleep. Try reading a book or listening to soothing music before bed instead.

3. Create a Calm Sleep Environment: Keep your room dark, quiet, and cool. Limit distractions like noise and light that can interfere with your sleep.

4. Exercise Regularly: Physical activity can help you sleep better. Just make sure not to exercise too close to bedtime as it may keep you awake.

5. Eat Healthy: What you eat can affect how well you sleep. Try to avoid heavy meals and caffeine close to bedtime.

Sleep is not a luxury, but a necessity for your body and mind to function optimally. Make it a priority, and you'll see a difference in your academic performance, mood, and overall well-being.

Journal Exercise:

1. Write about a time you didn't get enough sleep. How did it affect your mood, energy, and attention in school the next day?

2. Try adopting a new, healthier sleep routine for a week based on what you learned in this chapter. Write about the changes you made and how it affected your daily life.

☆ 6.3 ESTABLISHING HEALTHY DAILY ROUTINES

Amidst all the changes of puberty, one thing that can help keep you steady and strong is establishing healthy daily routines. Think of these routines as your personal lifeboat in the wild ocean of puberty. They're your constant, your anchor, helping you navigate the sometimes choppy waters. They'll support you in maintaining your physical health and emotional well-being, making your journey through puberty a smoother, more enjoyable ride.

Let's take a journey through an average day, exploring how healthy routines can be woven into your life. We'll follow a girl named Sophie and see what she does to establish her routines.

Sophie knows that mornings are important, so she has developed a routine to kickstart her day positively. She wakes up, makes her bed, and does simple stretching exercises. This gets her muscles moving and wakes up her body for the day. After brushing her teeth, she spends a few minutes in front of the mirror. Instead of focusing on any perceived flaws, Sophie reminds herself of her strengths. She says things like "I am strong," "I am capable," and "I am beautiful just the way I am." This affirming routine fosters a positive body image.

Sophie then moves on to her breakfast routine. She helps her mom prepare a balanced meal with fruits, proteins, and grains. Even as she eats, she makes it a point to appreciate the nourishment her food provides. This is not just about physical health, but emotional stability too. Associating food with positivity prevents unhealthy attitudes towards eating. School time for Sophie is about learning, but she also uses it to practice emotional stability. During breaks, instead of joining in gossip or negativity, Sophie practices mindfulness. She takes a few minutes to breathe deeply and focus on positive thoughts. This simple routine helps her stay emotionally balanced, even when school gets stressful.

After school, Sophie has her hygiene and self-care routines. She washes her hands regularly and showers after her extracurricular activities. She also devotes time to care for her changing body, using appropriate products for her skin type. Plus, homework is not just about getting it done for Sophie. She uses this time to practice discipline and focus - key ingredients of a healthy routine. Sophie doesn't forget about the importance of maintaining a healthy body image in the evening. While doing her skincare routine before bed, she repeats her positive affirmations. This consistent focus on positivity helps her foster a stronger, more resilient self-image. Finally, Sophie prepares for bedtime. She avoids electronic devices for at least an hour before sleep, opting for a book instead. Then, she takes a few moments to reflect on her day, jotting down three things she's grateful for in a journal.

This routine not only helps her fall asleep faster but also ends her day on a positive note.

Sophie's daily routines might look a little like this:

1. Start the day with stretching exercises followed by positive affirmations.

2. A nutritious breakfast and a moment of gratitude.

3. Mindfulness breaks during school hours.

4. After-school hygiene and homework routines.

5. Positive affirmations while getting ready for bed.

6. An hour of electronics-free time before listing down things she's grateful for.

Your routines might look different, and that's perfectly okay. The important thing is to create routines that support good hygiene, emotional stability, and a healthy body image.

Here are some exercises to help you build your own routines:

★ Create a list of positive affirmations that resonate with you. Practice saying them every morning and night.

★ Plan a balanced breakfast for the whole week. Pay attention to how these meals make you feel.

★ Identify two times during your school day when you can practice mindfulness. It can be as simple as closing your eyes and taking deep breaths.

★ Decide on a skincare routine that suits your needs. This could involve using a gentle cleanser and moisturizer.

★ Choose an activity to replace screen time before bed. It could be reading, drawing, or writing in a gratitude journal.

By practicing these exercises, you can start creating routines that work for you and support your growth. Remember, healthy routines are all about consistency. Don't worry if you miss a day; just pick up where you left off. The important thing is that you're trying, and with each day, you're taking steps towards becoming the best version of yourself.

Journal Exercise:

Write about the routines you would like to include in your daily lives from the chapter we just read. How do you think these new routines will benefit you? What challenges do you think you might face and how might you overcome them?

Chapter 7
COMMUNICATION AND SUPPORT

☆ 7.1 HOW TO TALK TO PARENTS AND GUARDIANS

When you change during puberty, things can feel quite overwhelming sometimes. Everything is new, it's like you stepped in a unknown world, and you sometimes feel as if you don't really know how to handle things. One of the best ways to deal with these changes is by having open and honest conversations with your parents or guardians. They can be a source of comfort, guidance, and information as you navigate these exciting yet challenging times. It's common to feel a little shy or uncomfortable when you want to talk about puberty. However, remember that your parents or guardians were once your age too, and they've experienced these changes first-hand. They can share their own experiences, provide reassurances, and help you better understand what's happening to your body and mind. So, though it may feel a bit awkward at first, it's crucial to communicate openly with them.

Here are a few reasons why open communication is so important during this time:

☆ Understanding: Your parents or guardians can help you understand the changes your body is going through. They can explain things in a way that's easy to understand and reassure you that what you're experiencing is normal.

★ Support: Experiencing puberty can sometimes feel lonely, but it's important to remember that you're not alone. Your parents or guardians are there for you. They can provide emotional support and comfort when you need it.

★ Guidance: As you experience new things and emotions, your parents or guardians can provide guidance on how to navigate these changes. They can help you make sense of your feelings and suggest strategies for dealing with challenging situations.

Now, you might wonder, "how do I start these conversations?". One effective strategy is to find a quiet and comfortable space where you can talk openly and without interruptions. Think about what you want to discuss ahead of time and consider how to express your thoughts and feelings in a way that feels genuine to you. It's okay if you don't have all the words or if you're not sure how to express what you're feeling. The important thing is to make an effort to open up and share. And remember, there's no rush. Take your time and speak at your own pace. You could even write down your thoughts or questions ahead of time if that feels easier. It's okay to have different conversations over time. You don't need to talk about everything all at once. You can start with a topic that feels comfortable to you and then gradually move on to other topics as you feel ready. The main goal is to maintain an ongoing dialogue about the changes you're experiencing, so you feel supported and understood throughout your journey into adolescence.

Let's jump into a few exercises, scenarios, and examples that can help you enhance your communication skills, overcome your fears about puberty-related conversations, and foster a better understanding between you and your parents or guardians.

1. Empathy Exercise: It's important to remember that your parents or guardians were once your age, experiencing similar feelings and changes. Try putting yourself in their

shoes. Draw or write down what you imagine they felt when they were going through puberty. This can help you appreciate their perspective and make it easier to talk to them about your experiences.

2. Role-playing: Role-play is a great way to practice your communication skills. Set aside some time with a close friend, sibling, or even a stuffed animal to practice these conversations. You'll play the role of yourself and your friend (or stuffed animal) will play the role of your parent or guardian. Start by expressing your concerns, feelings, or questions about puberty. Also, try to anticipate what your parent or guardian might say in response, and think about how you might react. For instance, you could start with something like:

You: "Mom, I've been noticing some changes in my body recently, and it's making me a bit uncomfortable."

'Mom': "I understand, sweetheart. Puberty can be a bit confusing, but it's a normal part of growing up. What changes are you talking about?"

Role-playing these conversations can help you feel more prepared and less anxious about the real thing.

3. Letter Writing Exercise: If you're having a hard time talking about puberty directly, writing a letter can be a useful way to express your feelings. In your letter, you can detail the changes you're experiencing, the fears or worries you have, and the questions you want to ask. Don't rush the process; take your time. Once you have completed your letter, you can decide if you want to give it to your parents or guardians or use it as a guide for a future conversation.

4. Question Jar: Create a question jar filled with questions you have about puberty. You and your parent or guardian can take turns pulling a question out of the jar and

discussing it. This can make the conversation feel less formal and more like a fun activity. Here are a few example questions you could use:

★ What happens during a period?

★ Why do I need to wear a bra?

★ Why is my body changing?

★ What should I expect during puberty?

5. Feelings Chart: Create a feelings chart where you can track your different emotions each day. If you feel comfortable, share this chart with your parents or guardians. This can help them understand how you're feeling and provide them with an opportunity to offer support.

6. Family Meeting: Suggest having a family meeting where you can openly talk about puberty and the changes you're going through. This can be a safe and open space for everyone to share their thoughts, feelings, and experiences. Remember, it's okay if you don't have all the answers. The purpose of these conversations is to understand and support each other better.

Opening up about puberty with your parents or guardians can be a little scary at first, but remember they are there to guide and support you. These exercises, role-playing scenarios, and practical examples can help you express your feelings better, ask necessary questions, and create a supportive dialogue about puberty. You're not alone in this journey, and the adults in your life are there to help you navigate through it.

Journal Exercise:

1. Write down two things that make you feel nervous or uncomfortable when talking about puberty to your parents/guardians.

2. Identify one adult you trust and feel comfortable talking to about your concerns and changes related to puberty. What makes you comfortable to talk to them?

3. Imagine a situation where you need to speak to your parents or guardians about puberty. Write down a few sentences or a short dialogue on how you plan to initiate the conversation.

4. Reflect on a time when you had a successful open conversation with your parents/guardians. What made it successful and how did it make you feel?

☆ 7.2 SEEKING SUPPORT FROM TEACHERS AND COUNSELORS

Your teachers and school counselors are there to provide support during the new period of your life of puberty. They are like your guides in this journey and are equipped with the knowledge and understanding to help you navigate through the labyrinth of puberty. Teachers do not just impart academic knowledge but also provide guidance and support on other aspects of life. They've seen and helped many other students through the very changes you're experiencing now. Similarly, school counselors are specifically trained to assist students with emotional, social, and psychological concerns. Think of them as your roadmap, leading you through the confusing pathways of puberty, and helping you understand and make sense of the changes happening to your body and mind.

Now, you might be wondering, "But how do I approach my teachers or counselors? What if they don't understand what I'm going through?" Remember, these individuals are professionals who have a deep understanding of the changes that puberty brings. They can offer advice, lend a listening ear, and guide you through any challenges you might be facing. Here are some ways you can approach teachers and counselors for assistance:

1. Schedule a meeting: Most schools have an open-door policy, meaning you can simply walk in and ask for help. However, if you feel more comfortable, you can also schedule a meeting to ensure you have dedicated time to talk.

2. Be honest: Teachers and counselors are there to help, but they can only do so if they know what's going on. Try to be as honest and open as possible about your concerns or experiences. It might feel scary at first to bare your emotions, but remember, they are there to support you.

3. Ask questions: Don't be afraid to ask questions. Puberty can be confusing, and it's natural to need clarity. Whether it's about physical changes, emotional shifts, or social situations, your teachers and counselors can provide the answers you're seeking.

4. Show gratitude: After discussing your concerns, remember to thank your teachers or counselors for their time and assistance. This demonstrates respect and appreciation for their efforts.

Remember, everyone's experience with puberty is different, and it's okay to seek help. There's no one-size-fits-all when it comes to growing up, and that's perfectly fine. Your teachers and counselors are there to support you, every step of the way.

So, don't be shy to reach out to them when you need support, advice, or just someone to listen.

ROLE	HOW THEY CAN HELP
Teachers	Guidance on academic challenges and social issues at school
School Counselors	Private conversations about personal or academic stresses
Career Counselors	Assist in planning future educational and career paths
Health Educators	Provide information about physical changes and health issues
Coaches	Mentorship in teamwork and personal discipline
Music or Art Teachers	Support in exploring creativity and expressing emotions

Imagine this: You're sitting in math class, and the teacher is explaining a new concept. You're trying your best to understand, but it just isn't making sense. You look around the room at your classmates, and they all seem to get it. You start to feel worried. What do you do? Here's a possible solution: After class, you could approach your teacher and say, "I'm having a hard time understanding this concept. Could we maybe go over it again, or could you suggest other resources I could use to understand it better?" That's an example of reaching out to your teacher for support.

Here are some tips on how to make this situation easier:

☆ Prepare what you're going to say beforehand. This way, you won't forget to mention any details that are important.

☆ Plan when you're going to talk to them. It could be after class, during a break, or maybe you could even send them an email.

☆ Be honest about what you're finding difficult. It's okay to admit you're struggling. That's the first step in getting the help you need.

In another scenario, imagine you're feeling really anxious about a big test coming up. You've been studying, but no amount of preparation seems to calm your nerves. You can't sleep properly, you're not eating well, and it's starting to affect your daily life. What can you do in this situation? You could reach out to a school counselor. You might say something like, "I'm feeling really stressed about an upcoming test and it's affecting my sleep and appetite. Could we talk about strategies to manage my anxiety?"

Not every situation where you could seek help from a teacher or counselor is academic or school-related. Let's say you're having a disagreement with a friend, and it's making you feel upset and confused. You're not sure how to resolve this disagreement, and it's starting to affect your schoolwork. This could be a perfect opportunity to seek advice from a teacher or counselor. During your meeting, you might say something like, "I've been having a hard time with a friend and it's starting to distract me from my schoolwork. Could we discuss this problem, and maybe you could give me some advice on how to handle it?" Here are a few practical tips for this situation:

☆ Choose a teacher or counselor who you trust and feel comfortable with. This could be a teacher from your favorite subject or a counselor you've talked to before.

★ Explain the situation clearly. Make sure you provide all the necessary details so they can understand the problem fully.

★ Ask for advice. They might provide you with some strategies on how to handle the situation, or they may offer to mediate a conversation between you and your friend.

In each of these scenarios, it's essential to remember that it's okay to ask for help. Everyone struggles at times, and teachers and counselors are there to help you navigate these challenges. They can provide support, resources, and advice, so don't be afraid to reach out to them.

Journal Exercise:

Reflect on a time when you had to seek support from a teacher or counselor. How did it make you feel? Write about the experience and the steps you took. Was there something specific you learned from that experience? How can this lesson help you in the future? If you had a magic wand, what would you do differently now?

Choose a teacher or counselor who you trust and consider how you might approach them when going through changes or challenges. What words would you use? Write a pretend letter to your chosen adult expressing your feelings and thoughts.

☆ 7.3 FINDING THE COURAGE TO ASK FOR HELP

As you grow and change, there will be times when you may need a little extra help. It's completely normal and nothing to be ashamed of. It's important to recognize when to ask for help during this time, and also to know that it's okay to do so. When intense feelings start to become too much to handle, or if they are causing distress or concern, it might be a sign that you need to reach out for help. It's important to listen to your feelings and your body. If something doesn't feel right, it's best to talk to someone about it. It's also important to remember that everyone needs help sometimes, and asking for it doesn't mean you're weak or incapable. In fact, it takes a lot of courage to admit when you're struggling and to ask for the help you need. This courage comes from within ourselves and is something we can all nurture and grow.

But how do we foster this courage? There are a few ways:

⭐ Practice self-compassion: Remember that it's okay to not be okay sometimes. Be kind to yourself, and give yourself permission to ask for help when you need it.

⭐ Open up to trusted people in your life: This could be a parent, a teacher, a school counselor, or a close friend. Share your feelings with them, and let them know if you're struggling.

⭐ Try to overcome fears of judgment: It's completely normal to worry about what others might think. But remember, everyone needs help sometimes, and there's no shame in asking for it.

⭐ Believe in your ability to get through tough times: You are stronger than you think and you have overcome challenges before. You can do it again.

Asking for help isn't always easy, but it's a crucial step in navigating the challenges of puberty. It's a sign of strength and bravery, and it's an essential part of taking care of your emotional health and well-being. Imagine this: you're working on a group project for school. You've been assigned to create a presentation on a topic you don't completely understand, and it's due in just a few days. Your classmates are relying on you, but you're feeling completely lost and stressed. What do you do in a situation like this? You ask for help, of course!

Let's see how we can navigate through this situation.

1. Identifying the Problem: Realize that it's okay to admit to yourself that there's something you don't understand. It's the first step towards finding a solution. In our scenario, the problem is that you don't fully understand the topic for your presentation.

2. Who to Ask: Once you've identified the problem, the next step is to figure out who can help you. Your teacher, who assigned the project, would be a great start. They already know what the project is about, and their job is to guide students, so they should be able to help you understand the topic better.

3. Preparing Your Question: Before you ask for help, it's important to prepare. Think about what exactly you need assistance with. In this case, you might need clarification on certain aspects of the topic, or help finding resources for your research.

4. Approaching the Person: When you ask for help, it's important to be polite and respectful. You could say something like, "Excuse me, I'm having a bit of trouble understanding this topic. Could you please help me out?"

Now, let's practice this with a role-playing exercise. Imagine your favorite teddy bear or doll is the teacher. Using the tips above, practice asking them for help. Pay attention to how you feel during this exercise. Do you feel nervous, embarrassed, or confident? Remember, it's normal to feel a mix of emotions when asking for help. With time and practice, it'll feel more natural and less daunting.

Another everyday situation could be at home. Picture this: you're trying to learn a new dance routine for a school event, but one particular move is giving you a hard time. You've watched the video tutorial over and over again, but you just can't get it right. So, what do you do?

1. Identifying the Problem: The tricky dance move is the issue here.

2. Who to Ask: Perhaps you have a friend or sibling who's good at dancing. They could be your go-to person for help.

3. Preparing Your Question: Be specific about what you're struggling with. You might say, "I can't seem to get the timing for this spin right. Can you show me how?"

4. Approaching the Person: Approach them politely and ask if they have some time to help you out.

You can also practice this scenario through role-play. Use a stuffed animal or action figure as your 'dancer' friend and ask them for help. You can use this four-step process anytime you're facing a difficulty and need assistance. The most important thing to remember is that asking for help is not a sign of weakness; it's a sign of courage and determination. Everyone needs help at times. Furthermore, seeking assistance often leads to stronger relationships with the people around you, as they see your dedication to learning and growth. So don't be afraid to speak up when you need help. You're not alone in this journey, and there are many people ready and willing to lend a hand.

Journal Exercise:

1. List three moments or situations where you felt you needed help but did not ask for it. Write a brief sentence describing each moment.

2. Now, for each moment you have described, and reflect on your feelings during that time. How did it feel to hold back from asking for help? Write this down too.

3. Choose one of these situations. Pretend you could go back to this moment with the knowledge and courage you have now. Write down how you would ask for help in that scenario.

4. Reflect on the consequences. How different do you think the outcome would have been if you had asked for help?

5. Thinking about the future, write down three affirmations that will encourage you to ask for help when you need it.

Chapter 8
NAVIGATING MISINFORMATION

☆ 8.1 ADDRESSING COMMON MYTHS

In a world full of information, it's easy to come across myths and misconceptions, especially about puberty. It's important to separate fact from fiction so you can understand your body and its changes accurately and healthily. Here, we'll address some common myths you might hear about puberty and explain why they aren't true.

Myth I: Puberty Starts at the Same Age for Everyone

> ★ Truth: The start of puberty varies for each person. While it often begins between ages 8 and 14, it's perfectly normal to start earlier or later. Everyone's body has its own schedule.

Myth 2: You're Not Normal if You Don't Look Like Your Friends

> ★ Truth: Everyone's body is unique and develops at its own pace. Comparing yourself to friends or images in the media isn't a fair comparison. Embrac e your body's changes at your own pace.

Myth 3: Menstruation is Dirty or Shameful

> ★ Truth: Menstruation is a natural and healthy part of being a girl. It's a sign your body is working correctly and maturing. There's nothing dirty or shameful about it.

Myth 4: You Can't Get Pregnant During Your Period

> ★ Truth: While it's less likely, it is still possible to get pregnant during your period. Understanding your menstrual cycle is an important part of puberty education.

Myth 5: Wearing a Bra Stops Your Breasts from Growing

> ★ Truth: Wearing a bra doesn't affect how your breasts grow. Bras are meant to support your breasts, especially during physical activities, but they don't influence growth.

Myth 6: If You Don't Have a Growth Spurt, You Won't Grow Tall

> ★ Truth: Growth during puberty varies. Some girls have a noticeable growth spurt, while others grow gradually. Your

final height is determined by genetics and overall health, not just your growth pattern during puberty.

Myth 7: Eating Certain Foods Will Speed Up Puberty

★ Truth: No specific food can speed up or delay puberty. A balanced diet is important for your overall health and can support normal development, but it won't drastically change your body's natural timing for puberty.

Myth 8: Only Girls Have Emotional Changes During Puberty

★ Truth: Emotional changes during puberty are not exclusive to girls. Boys also experience a range of emotional shifts due to hormonal changes. It's normal for both girls and boys to feel mood swings, heightened emotions, or even confusion during this time.

Myth 9: You Must Start Shaving as Soon as You Hit Puberty

★ Truth: The decision to start shaving is a personal one and isn't dictated by a specific age or stage of puberty. Some girls choose to shave body hair for personal or cultural reasons, while others do not. It's a matter of personal preference and comfort.

Myth 10: Acne is Caused by Dirty Skin

★ Truth: Acne during puberty is primarily caused by hormonal changes that increase oil production in the skin, not necessarily by dirt or poor hygiene. While good skin care is important, acne is a normal part of puberty for many and can occur even with diligent hygiene.

Myth 11: If You Don't Have a Period by Age 12, There's Something Wrong

★ Truth: The age at which girls start menstruating can vary widely. Some girls get their first period as early as 8 or 9, while others might not start menstruating until they are 15 or 16. This wide range is considered normal.

Myth 12: Physical Development is the Only Important Aspect of Puberty

★ Truth: While physical changes are the most noticeable signs of puberty, they are not the only aspect. Emotional, mental, and social development are also crucial parts of puberty. Developing a healthy body image, learning to manage emotions, and building social skills are all important components of this developmental stage.

★ 8.2 SORTING FACT FROM FICTION

Now, how can we train our minds to distinguish between fact and fiction? Let's try a simple exercise.

1. Next time you hear a piece of information, pause and ask yourself, „Where did this come from?" Is it a trusted source like a doctor, parent, or teacher? Or is it just a rumor from a friend or something you read on the internet?

2. Then ask, "Does this seem logical?" Use your own knowledge and common sense to assess the information.

3. Finally, "Can I verify this?" Try to find a reliable source that can confirm or refute the information you've heard.

4. Let's put this into practice with an everyday situation. Imagine you overhear a conversation at school where a classmate says that, "Shaving makes hair grow back thicker." You remember the exercise and start questioning.

„Where did this come from?" You realize the source is a classmate, not necessarily a reliable source.

1. "Does this seem logical?" You think about it and it doesn't quite make sense to you. How would cutting hair on the surface of the skin affect how it grows from the follicle under the skin?

2. "Can I verify this?" When you get home, you ask your mom, a trusted adult, and she explains that this is a common myth. Hair might seem thicker after shaving because it's cut at a blunt angle, but it doesn't actually change the thickness or growth rate.

By asking these questions, you've debunked the myth, replacing it with fact!

Remember, it's okay to not know everything about puberty, and it's perfectly fine to have questions.

MYTH	REALITY
You stop growing after puberty	Growth can continue into the late teens and early twenties
Periods are extremely painful for everyone	Pain levels vary person to person and can be managed
Boys mature faster than girls	Girls typically start puberty earlier than boys
You'll definitely get acne during puberty	Not everyone experiences acne

MYTH	REALITY
Only women experience mood swings during puberty	Hormonal changes can cause mood swings in both genders
You should feel attracted to boys in puberty	It's normal to experience attraction to any gender during puberty

Chapter 9
FURTHER RESOURCES AND GUIDANCE

☆ 9.1 RECOMMENDED READING AND WEBSITES

This chapter aims to provide a list of resources specifically beneficial for girls going through puberty. These resources include books and websites that offer reliable information, advice, and support on various aspects related to physical, emotional, and mental changes during adolescence.

Books:

1. „The Care and Keeping of You: The Body Book for Younger Girls" by Valorie Schaefer - This book is a favorite among preteens for its clear, age-appropriate information about the physical changes that girls experience.

2. "It's Perfectly Normal: Changing Bodies, Growing Up, Sex, and Sexual Health" by Robie H. Harris - A comprehensive and respectful guide that covers a wide range of topics including body development and sexual health.

3. "The Feelings Book: The Care & Keeping of Your Emotions" by Dr. Lynda Madison - Focused on the emotional aspects of puberty, this book offers insights and advice on handling the wide range of feelings and moods that come with adolescence.

Websites:

1. KidsHealth.org - A reliable source for health information for kids and teens, offering easy-to-understand articles about puberty and other health-related topics.

2. GirlsHealth.gov - Run by the U.S. Department of Health and Human Services, this site provides girls with information about health, relationships, and growing up.

3. YoungWomensHealth.org - A resource provided by the Boston Children's Hospital offering health information for teen girls around the world, including detailed sections on puberty and mental health.

Online Platforms:

1. Planned Parenthood Teen Talk - A safe and moderated online space for teens to talk about health, sex, and relationships. It provides accurate and judgment-free information.

2. TeenHealthFX.com - An online resource for adolescents, providing comprehensive health and lifestyle information, including aspects of puberty and development.

3. Amaze.org - Offers engaging, informative, and age-appropriate animated videos that explain different aspects of puberty, sexual health, and relationships.

YouTube Channels:

1. Sexplanations - Hosted by Dr. Lindsey Doe, this channel provides open discussions about sex education and puberty in an informative and accessible manner.

2. TED-Ed - Offers a range of educational videos, including several on human biology and the science behind puberty, presented in an engaging format.

It's essential to have open and honest discussions about these topics. These resources can provide valuable information, but it's also important to talk with trusted adults like parents, guardians, or healthcare providers for personalized advice and support.

☆ 9.2 ACCESSING SUPPORT NETWORKS AND HELPLINES

Navigating through puberty can be challenging, and it's important to know where to find additional support and guidance. This section lists various support networks and helplines that are available to help girls understand and cope with the changes they are experiencing during adolescence. These resources offer confidential advice and are staffed by professionals trained in adolescent development and mental health.

Support Networks:

1. Girl Scouts of the USA - This organization provides a supportive community for girls to learn about health, personal development, and leadership. They often have programs specifically addressing issues related to puberty and adolescence.

2. Girls Inc. - An organization dedicated to empowering young girls to be strong, smart, and bold. They offer mentorship and various programs focusing on the unique challenges faced by girls during their developmental years.

3. Boys & Girls Clubs of America - While inclusive of all genders, this organization offers a variety of programs that help young people develop self-esteem and learn about their changing bodies and emotions.

Helplines:

1. National Suicide Prevention Lifeline (1-800-273-TALK) - Provides 24/7, free, and confidential support for people in distress, prevention and crisis resources. This helpline is crucial for addressing emotional and mental health issues that can arise during puberty.

2. Crisis Text Line (Text HOME to 741741) - A free, 24/7 text line for people in crisis. Volunteers offer support for those dealing with mental health difficulties, including issues related to puberty.

3. Teen Line (1-800-TLC-TEEN) - A teen-to-teen helpline with community outreach services, providing a safe space for teenagers to talk about their problems, including those related to puberty and growing up.

Online Communities:

1. 7 Cups for Teens - An online platform where teens can anonymously connect with trained volunteer listeners in chat rooms to talk about any issues they're facing, including puberty.

2. ReachOut Forums - Part of the ReachOut USA network, these forums offer a safe and supportive online space where teens can share their experiences and support each other through various challenges, including those related to puberty.

Local Resources:

☆ Check local community centers, schools, and health clinics for additional resources. Many communities have programs or counselors who specialize in youth and adolescent health.

Access to the right support can make a big difference in how you navigate the challenges of puberty. Remember, it's okay to ask for help, and reaching out is a sign of strength. Whether it's a question about physical changes, emotional struggles, or just needing someone to talk to, these resources are here to assist you.

CONCLUSION

☆ 10.1 EMBRACING YOUR UNIQUE JOURNEY

As we reach the end of our guide, it's important to remember that puberty is a unique journey for every girl. Just like snowflakes, no two experiences are exactly alike, and that's perfectly okay! Your body, your emotions, and your experiences are yours alone, and they make you special and unique.

Celebrate Your Individuality: You might notice changes in your body at a different time than your friends, and that's normal. Whether you're the first in your class to need a bra or the last one to get your period, each of these milestones is a part of your personal journey. Embrace these differences - they make you who you are.

Understand That Changes Are Normal: It's completely natural to feel a mix of excitement and uncertainty during this time. Remember, everyone goes through it, and it's okay to have lots of questions. This guide, along with the resources in Chapter 9, can be your companions whenever you need some advice or reassurance.

Talk About Your Feelings: It's good to talk about what you're going through, whether it's with your family, friends, or a trusted adult like a teacher or school counselor. Sharing your thoughts and feelings can help you feel supported and understood.

Be Kind to Yourself: This time of change is not just about your body, but also about your emotions. Be gentle with yourself. It's okay to feel happy, sad, confused, or excited - sometimes all in one day!

Stay Positive and Curious: Puberty is not just about the challenges; it's also an exciting time of growth and learning. Stay curious about the world and your place in it. Keep exploring your interests, whether it's in sports, arts, science, or reading.

You're not alone on this journey. There are so many people who care about you and are ready to support you. Embrace your unique path and know that it's leading you to an exciting future.

☆ 10.2 LOOKING FORWARD WITH CONFIDENCE

As you grow and move through the journey of puberty, it's important to look towards the future with confidence. This chapter is about carrying the lessons, understanding, and self-awareness you've gained through this guide into your future years. Here are some key points to help you step forward with confidence:

Build on Your Strengths: You have many wonderful qualities and strengths, some of which you're just beginning to discover. Focus on what you do well and what makes you feel good about yourself. Whether it's being a great friend, excelling in a subject at school, or being talented in a sport or art, these strengths are part of what makes you amazing.

Stay Curious and Keep Learning: There is so much more to learn - not just about puberty, but about the world around you. Keep asking questions, seeking information, and trying new things. The more you know, the more confident you'll feel in making decisions about your life.

Take Care of Your Health: Physical, mental, and emotional health are all important. Eating healthy foods, getting enough sleep, exercising, and finding ways to handle stress are all part of taking care of yourself. When you feel good physically, you're more likely to feel confident and happy.

Set Goals for Yourself: Think about what you want to achieve in the next few years. It could be academic goals, personal improvement goals, or even just fun activities you want to try. Setting goals gives you something to aim for and helps you stay motivated.

Believe in Yourself: You are capable of achieving great things. Believe in your abilities, trust in your own judgment, and don't be afraid to stand up for what you believe in. Self-belief is a powerful tool that will guide you through many challenges.

Seek Support When You Need It: Remember, asking for help is a sign of strength, not weakness. If you're ever unsure, confused, or just need someone to talk to, turn to the people and resources you trust.

Be Kind to Others and Yourself: Treat others with kindness and respect, and remember to be kind to yourself too. Everyone is going through their own journey, and a little kindness can make a big difference.

As you grow and change, keep these thoughts in mind. With each passing day, you're becoming the wonderful person you're meant to be. Embrace the future with excitement and confidence, knowing that you have the tools and support to navigate whatever comes your way. Remember, your journey is unique, and you have the strength and courage to make it a beautiful one.

DISCLAIMER

This book, "The Complete Girls' Guide to Puberty: Understanding Your Evolving Body, Mind, and Feelings During Growth," is intended as a resource to provide information and guidance for girls aged 8-12 as they navigate the transformative journey of puberty. It is important to note that the content within this book is for informational purposes only and does not substitute for professional medical advice, diagnosis, or treatment.

While every effort has been made to ensure the accuracy and relevance of the information presented, individual experiences may vary, and it is recommended that readers consult with qualified healthcare professionals or trusted adults for personalized advice regarding their specific health and well-being. The author and publisher disclaim any liability or responsibility for any adverse effects or consequences resulting directly or indirectly from the use of information contained in this book.

Additionally, parents and guardians are encouraged to review the content of this book before sharing it with their children to ensure its appropriateness for their unique circumstances and beliefs. The book is designed to open a positive and informed dialogue between girls and their caregivers about puberty, and it is essential to approach these conversations with sensitivity, understanding, and empathy.

Readers are urged to use their discretion and judgment when applying the advice and recommendations presented in this book, recognizing that every individual is unique and may require tailored guidance. Ultimately, this book is intended to empower and educate young girls, fostering a healthy and informed approach to their evolving bodies and emotions during the puberty years.

Made in the USA
Coppell, TX
05 August 2024

35454194R00080